B L A C K

T0015542

A G A I N

of related interest

Overcoming Everyday Racism
Building Resilience and Wellbeing in the Face of
Discrimination and Microaggressions
Susan Cousins
ISBN 978 1 78592 850 5
eISBN 978 1 78592 851 2

My Black Motherhood
Mental Health, Stigma, Racism and the System
Sandra Igwe
ISBN 978 1 83997 008 5
eISBN 978 1 83997 009 2

Black and Menopausal
Intimate Stories of Navigating the Change
Edited by Yansie Rolston and Yvonne Christie
Foreword by Iya Rev. DeShannon Barnes-Bowens, M.S.
ISBN 978 1 83997 379 6
eISBN 978 1 83997 380 2

Black, Brilliant and Dyslexic
Neurodivergent Heroes Tell their Stories
Edited by Marcia Brissett-Bailey
Foreword by Atif Choudhury
ISBN 978 1 83997 133 4
eISBN 978 1 83997 134 1

White Privilege Unmasked
How to Be Part of the Solution
Judy Ryde
ISBN 978 1 78592 408 8
eISBN 978 1 78450 767 1

BLACK *Again*

Losing and Reclaiming My Racial Identity
LATONYA SUMMERS

Jessica Kingsley Publishers
London and Philadelphia

First published in Great Britain in 2024 by Jessica Kingsley Publishers
An imprint of John Murray Press

1

Copyright © LaTonya Summers 2024

The right of LaTonya Summers to be identified as the Author of the
Work has been asserted by her in accordance with the Copyright,
Designs and Patents Act 1988

Content Warning: This book mentions abuse, bullying, sexual assault
and racism.

A CIP catalogue record for this title is available from the
British Library and the Library of Congress

ISBN 978 1 83997 318 5
eISBN 978 1 83997 319 2

Printed and bound in Great Britain by Clays Ltd

Jessica Kingsley Publishers' policy is to use papers that are natural,
renewable and recyclable products and made from wood grown
in sustainable forests. The logging and manufacturing processes
are expected to conform to the environmental regulations
of the country of origin.

Jessica Kingsley Publishers
Carmelite House
50 Victoria Embankment
London EC4Y 0DZ

www.jkp.com

John Murray Press
Part of Hodder & Stoughton Limited
An Hachette UK Company

*To my four-year-old self, who waited patiently
for the return to my true Black self.*

Contents

Acknowledgements

I stopped writing a few years after my novel *Good To Me* was published. I started several manuscripts but for whatever reasons I could not complete them. Brother Ali, my dad who is an author himself, called it "sophomore jinx." But this book showed me that I'd not only lost my voice, but also myself. I believed I did not have anything to say that anybody would want to hear. Therefore, I would like to acknowledge a few people who led me to find myself and my voice and to use both for good.

To Jane Evans at Jessica Kingsley Publishers for emailing me "out of the blue" with a challenge I couldn't say no to. Thank you for helping me break my silence.

To Nathan Summers and our six young adult children. Now you can stop counting the number of books I started and did not complete. But thank you for keeping count and always noticing. I love you.

To Brenda and Brother Ali for bringing me into this world and for keeping watch from the outside in. Thank you!

To Momma Lorraine and Daddy Charles: Thank you for EVERYTHING!

To Luck and Chuck for sharing your parents and lives with me. Thank you for loving me as your big sister so much that I forget life started for us as cousins. I love you.

To my co-workers at Jacksonville University for watching me blossom. Thank you for being great training grounds.

To Lavonne, April, and Kim for being the best girlfriends on this side of heaven. Thank you for being my village, even when I thought the other side was better.

To Drs. Leroy Baruth, Georgia Rhoades, Geri Miller, and Kate Brinko, former professors and supervisors of mine at Appalachian State University. Thank you for creating opportunities for me and mentoring and sponsoring me toward success.

Introduction

When I told Brother Ali, my biological father, that I was writing another book, he proudly reminded me that I had written my first novel when I was eight years old, and that it was called *Snowdrift*, about a Black girl wanting to be white. Fast forward 40 years and this book is about recovering from the traumatic process of losing and reclaiming my Blackness. I doubt at such a young age I knew the precise meaning of the word snowdrift—a mound of snow driven by the wind—but I'd say it is an apt word to describe myself having been driven by the belief that if I wanted to go *somewhere* I'd need to be something other than Black.

I know that last sentence might sting to some readers, especially those who are younger and growing up in a time where Blackness and authenticity are encouraged and celebrated. But it has not always been that way, at least not for me. I was born one generation after Jim Crowism ended (*shifted* would be a more accurate word) and am still impacted by direct and indirect messages that made Blackness more painful than beautiful.

But you'll read more about the things that interrupted my Blackness and finally the things that led me back to it.

Therefore, I chose to tell this story in three parts because I know it might be hard for some readers to understand how a person could lose their racial identity or why a person wouldn't want to be the race or ethnicity they were born into. I know it isn't easy to grasp how a dark-skinned woman such as myself could ever think I could *pass* for white but the mind is a powerful thing and mine will believe anything I tell it. Everybody's story is different—even those who know exactly what I'm talking about because their experiences are similar—so in Part 1, Losing Myself, I reflect on some painful experiences that made me believe that whiteness would lead to better living. There, I share my undoing—that which was done to me by Black hands, that which I permitted by white ones, and that which I did to myself. Nevertheless, I was determined to find and make a better life than the one I was handed, by any means necessary. What I didn't know was that the more white norms, values, and traditions I picked up, the more Black pieces of myself I dropped.

My hands were full of accomplishments which I saw as proof of the distance I had put between myself and my traumatic beginnings and evidence that whiteness seemed to be working for me—advanced education, home ownership in the suburbs, good credit, access to money, published books and articles, a local television show, enough awards to cover a wall, a quiver full of amazing children, and so on. That is not to say that I do not believe I could have obtained these things by being authentically Black, it's just that I did not know how to. Coming from where I did and being one of the first among my biological family members to graduate high school, not lose my children to foster care and the penitentiary system, and acquire homeownership, I did not have a blueprint and white people seemed to know the architects. A part of my recovery from assimilation has been accepting responsibility as the builder of my own life.

Honestly, I would still be trying to pass today if it were not for the news of Trayvon Martin's murder in 2012. I did not personally know Trayvon and still his death changed the trajectory of my racial identity development, leading me to see that living in white spaces was not a shield as I had presumed, but could be a hazardous sword. It was something about recognizing that Trayvon's youthful innocence was obscured by racist misperceptions about his gender, race, and hoodie that made me realize that me trying to pass was a moot point. Contrary to what I had come to believe, the world saw me as Black and I knew I needed to as well.

Part 2, Reclaiming Myself, chronicles a reckoning with the realization that letting go of the pain associated with my childhood did not mean I needed to let go of the roots that sustained me. It is painful to explore these things and admit them, but I write them with hope that any reader who stands at the crossroad of who they are and who they want to be does not choose the way of racial colorblindness, passing, or denying themselves and their people. Let my story be enough of a cautionary tale. Freedom from race-based pain did not come from denying my race, but through reclaiming my Blackness and becoming Black again.

Finally, Part 3, Living and Loving Myself, is an exploration of how negotiating my identities as a Black woman in white spaces required a reconciliation of my race and gender. After years of choosing, depending on circumstances, which was more salient—being Black or a woman—I realized that if I was going to live and love fully again I needed to learn to enter spaces wholly.

This book is written for three kinds of readers: the reader who has no idea why someone would assimilate, the reader who has wondered what life is like for those who assimilate, and the reader who is recovering from assimilation. What you will read is one person's journey through the continuum of racial identity development. We all traverse along the path of becoming who we are, and I believe we will do well to examine how racial identity impacts that process. At the end of racial identity development is anti-racism and inclusion, though sadly some of us never get there. I hope this book illuminates the path to wholeness so we recognize the different forms of racism—whether covert, overt, aversive, and even internalized. We are all in unique positions to help one another grow with grace, humility, and authenticity.

Part 1
LOSING MYSELF

CHAPTER 1

Blackness Interrupted

From a trauma-filled recollection, I recall my earliest interaction with white people. I was a four-year-old patient on the children's unit of a local hospital in Charlotte, North Carolina where two white teenage hospital volunteers, who were called candy stripers, sat at my bedside reading stories from a book to me. I remember them vividly—a girl and a boy, both with rosy cheeks and blond locks, wearing red and white striped aprons that made them look like human peppermint candy sticks. They were different from the young people I interacted with at home, mostly cousins and neighbors, as these adolescents laughed easily and walked completely unencumbered. Their visit was like a cool washcloth on my forehead as I lay there feverish from a sexually transmitted disease that older people got when they failed to protect themselves, or in my case when older people had failed to protect me. Eventually, my health was restored, through an entire team of white doctors, nurses, and candy stripers, with not one Black helping professional in sight. My young mind took in all those things and spun them around to make sense of them as well as words nobody bothered to explain such as *gonorrhea*, sexual *abuse*, *negligence*, *unfit*, and *foster care*.

I still remember Alden Davis, the white woman social worker who drove me to a house I did not recognize and left me to live with a white foster family. My first meal was a peanut butter and pancake syrup sandwich cut diagonally. I had only eaten peanut butter and jelly sandwiches on whole slices of bread, so the peanut butter with syrup meal was an odd concoction to me in more ways than one. I did not like it, but I did not have a choice. I had already learned by then to keep my mouth closed and to be grateful.

Although I cannot recall what it felt like to experience trauma, pain, shock, and dissonance all at once while being removed from a Black home and transplanted into a white one, I imagine that it jump-started my ability to deny what I saw and felt. The impact had to be great because one time as an adult, I opened the door to my food pantry to put back a jar of peanut butter my children had left on the table. In the split-second right before the pantry door closed, I caught a glimpse of the peanut butter jar sitting next to a bottle of Aunt Jemima pancake syrup. I froze. That one sight caused memories of my first foster care experience to flood me—being the only Black person in a white home and their church and me squeezing the hand of my white foster mother because of the way people stared at us in the grocery store. These things I'd forgotten pulled me down to the floor like a riptide. I sat there sobbing like a four-year-old who had lost her mother, with the phantom taste of a peanut butter and syrup sandwich on my tongue.

I wondered what the hospital's treatment team meeting had been like as they decided what the best next steps for me would be—did they consider a Black foster home and none were available or was there an implicit (or explicit) consensus that a white environment would better counterbalance all that I'd been through? If I had to pinpoint a place where my fascination with wanting to know the differences between how white and Black people lived began, I might stick a pin in the pain of this four-year-old experience.

It wasn't long before I was adopted by Grandma Louise, my biological father, Brother Ali's mother, who skillfully restored my sense of self with her tireless love and push for academics. Under her tutelage, I became a reading, writing, counting, and praying four-year-old. Soon, I was bussed to a predominantly white school, Plaza Road Elementary, where I skipped kindergarten and fell in love with my first-grade teacher Miss Woods, my peers, and learning. Miss Woods was a beautiful fair-skinned Black woman. She was tall, thin, and graceful. She had straight fine hair that she let me comb and run my fingers through. My first best friend was a white girl student from Miss Woods' class named Wendy whom I gave our home phone number to. One day Wendy called the house and Grandma Louise answered and handed the phone to me. I was so happy about receiving my first ever phone call that I didn't notice my grandmother's face, but after I finished my call she asked, "Was that a little white girl?" I wish I had seen her facial expression to know if she was proud, excited, or disappointed. The question could have meant that she was not used to non-Black people calling her home, or maybe she worried that my time in a white foster home had led me to a preference for white people. But my most educated guess is that she was afraid that school integration would lead me down the same road Brother

Ali, whom she had named Larry Eugene, had traveled—the school-to-prison pipeline.

Having grown up in all-Black communities, with Black-owned businesses, Black churches, and Black schools, Brother Ali flourished academically, socially, and emotionally. But when he was bussed from his community school to a predominantly white one, he told me that he found himself in classes with white teachers who presumed he was ignorant. He recalled being talked down to, ignored in class, and questioned about who had completed his work because presumably it was too well written to have come from him. He had learned sportsmanship and a village mentality in his community, but what he saw and was taught on the white school grounds and playing fields changed him. There, he was taught to win at all costs. He recounted how those conflicting messages and being looked down on affected his psyche to the point where he began rebelling. Before long, he would be found in detention, then jail, and eventually prison. In and out of maximum-security institutions, he found refuge in the teachings of the Honorable Elijah Muhammed and become a devout Muslim in the Nation of Islam. He legally changed his name to one that included three forenames with Ali as his surname. One time I heard a Muslim woman call him Brother Ali, which to me suited him and his look and I began using it. My father stood upright at an easy 6'5, kingly with his dark chocolate skin and locs tied together at his back, with the crown of his head covered in a black, green, yellow, and red-knit beanie. I thought he looked like Africa and freedom, a stark contradiction to a man who would spend 30 years locked away in America's prison cages. Perhaps Grandma Louise worried that I'd meet the same fate, that white schooling would untie my family roots and lead me down unfamiliar paths. Nevertheless, I knew Grandma Louise's question about who was on the other end of her phone was not a malicious one, because a lot of the conversations in her house were colored.

Grandma Louise and I did not live alone. My young Aunt Lorraine, her husband Charles, and their new baby girl Latasha whom we called Luck lived with us. In contrast to my home of origin, I remember good things about living with Grandma Louise—uninterrupted water and electricity, a fully stocked food pantry and refrigerator, a play room full of toys, a fish aquarium, music playing from the component set, friends up and down the street, neighbors who looked out for one another, a floor model television in the living room where we all sat together, dinners in the dining room (which we called *the den*), breakfasts at the kitchen table, and abundant Christmases. We had a huge Granny Smith apple tree in the backyard and sometimes we'd come home to find people in the tree shaking limbs to make the apples fall. Grandma Louise made apple pies from its harvest. Luck and I played in the backyard, enjoyed Grandma Louise's homemade ice cream on the back porch, and people-watched from the front porch. I was not a foster child in that home. However, after taking me in, Grandma Louise became a foster parent to Black and white children. I would not be surprised if she had learned that there were not many Black foster parents and she set out to change that.

We were the kind of family that packed the car up to go on Sunday drives. We loved driving though different communities, as Charlotte was and still is broken up into four sections—East Charlotte, North Charlotte where I had lived earlier with

Brenda, my biological mother, West Charlotte where Grandma Louise's house sat, and the predominantly white South Charlotte. I always knew when we arrived at South Charlotte because the entrances to its communities were tree-lined, its streets were wider than ours, the two- and three-level houses looked like mansions as opposed to the ranch houses on our street, and the grass was so green and shiny it looked like the stringy plastic grass Grandma Louise used to fill up my and Luck's Easter baskets. We oohed and aahed over the houses and Grandma would announce, "Yep, this is where the rich white people live," in much the same tone that she used when she asked about Wendy calling the house.

This is where the rich white people live. It would have been simple to accept that statement at face value, especially since South Charlotte was full of white people who had or appeared to have money. But as a precocious youngster, I interpreted that Grandma Louise had said two things: that Black people were not rich, and that Black people did not live in South Charlotte. I made up my mind to do both. When I grew up, I was going to one day live among the white people.

The first time I pretended to be white—at least that's how Grandma Louise interpreted it—I was six years old. I centered a yellow towel on my head and tossed it back and forth as if it was my hair. I got a whipping for that. When Grandma Louise and Aunt Lorraine administered what might now be called an *old-fashioned whipping*, where the whipper was lectured to the beat of the administered licks. It would go something like: "Didn't *pop* I *pop* tell *pop* you *pop* not to *pop* leave this *pop* house *pop* when I'm not home?" Thankfully, Grandma Louise wasn't long-winded, and I don't remember her exact words, but I do remember that her talk was an admonishment for not being proud to be Black.

I was proud of quite a few things: my intelligence, living at Grandma Louise's house, and being a good child. But being *Black* wasn't one of them. It didn't make sense to me to be proud of something I had not worked for. I thought I was supposed to be proud of stuff like getting good grades or winning awards, and not getting put out of people's foster homes. I wasn't ashamed of being Black, that I was aware of. Even though for me, being Black had been a source of pain not pride.

As a child I hated *Good Times*, the television show about the Evans family's life in the ghetto. Most episodes were filled with hope that they would get out of dire straits, only to have it end as a series of failed opportunities. Many days of the week, we'd gather around the floor model television in the living room and watch Grandma Louise's favorite shows: *The Lawrence Welk Show*, *Hee Haw*, *All in the Family*, and on one evening, *Good Times* would be followed by *The Jeffersons*. The few minutes of space between the Evans family and the Jeffersons was not enough time for me to cognitively process how Black people could live such vastly different lives. I needed more time to adjust going from one theme song to another. How, in three minutes, could I recover from *keeping your head above water* to the other's proud pronouncement of *well, we're movin' on up*? Even then it was mind-boggling to my primary-school-aged self as I considered the stark contrasts between the two families' clothing, hairstyles, and way of living. Both families lived in apartments, but the Jeffersons had a doorman, a maid, a business, and friends who were as rich as they were. I did not know anyone who lived like them.

Ominously, a few days before my seventh birthday, Grandma Louise said to my Aunt Lorraine, "Let me go in here and bake this cake for Tonya's birthday. It might be the last one I bake." She baked me a yellow cake with chocolate frosting, still my favorite to this day. Grandma Louise died from cancer a day or so before my birthday. Our neighbor, Miss Margaret, came and got Luck and me while the paramedics were at the house. We were oblivious to what was going on, even while we watched the paramedics carry a stretcher with a white sheet-covered body out of the door, down the two sets of steps leading to the street, and into their ambulance. Miss Margaret wept, and Luck and I tried to keep our red popsicles from melting and getting on our clothes so Grandma Louise wouldn't fuss at us.

On the day of the funeral, Brenda, my biological mother, came over to the house to continue paying her respects. She was still dressed in black when she asked Aunt Lorraine if she could take me shopping for my birthday and get me some school clothes. I was happy that she said Luck could come too. Aunt Lorraine consented, as she was probably desperate for a break from the two of us since Grandma Louise *went to heaven* and was not around to take care of us. Brenda arrived the next day, and Luck and I climbed into her car. She drove us to a nearby Richway (a store like an upscale Kmart) and Luck and I circled racks of clothing, oohing and aahing over pink and sparkly shirts. Then out of the blue, my mother's sister showed up at the store. I had not seen her since I was four years old when she helped Brenda determine that I needed to be hospitalized for fever. I ran to her and gave her the biggest hug. I thought it was cool that she had come to help us pick out clothes. But no more than ten minutes later, the four of us left the store. Brenda and I loaded into her car, and my aunt helped Luck into my aunt's car. I replayed Aunt Lorraine's instructions to try and make sense of what was happening. *School shopping. Richway up the street. Me and Luck. Bring them right back.* Getting into separate cars did not feel as if it was part of the plan but it also didn't feel as if I was in danger. Maybe they did not see any clothes they liked for us, and Brenda was going to follow her sister back to my Aunt Lorraine's house. But Brenda and I sat there, watching my aunt and Luck drive away. Eventually, we left too and headed home, but to Brenda's house.

Under my mother's care, I switched schools so often that my peers did not get a chance to know me by name. They simply called me "Smart." At. Every. School. It started in second grade when I wrote a poem called "The Wind" (I must've had a thing for natural elements, considering a snowdrift then and now the wind) that a visiting teacher selected to use in her anthology. By third grade, I participated in spelling bees. In fourth grade, the teacher called me in front of the class to recite the nines row of the multiplication table, which I was able to do effortlessly because I realized that the first digit increased, and the second digit decreased in the succession of nines. The teacher was proud of me, but I didn't think that had anything to do with me being smart, I had just found a trick. In the middle of the school year, on my first day at a new school the sixth-grade teacher held up the test he'd administered and graded and said, "How come the new girl earned the highest test score on subject matter that y'all have been learning all week?" That did it, from then on out my classmates called me Smart.

Being smart got me recognized, advanced me. I loved earning awards for reading, writing, and good citizenship, and making achievements. Being smart, I learned how to survive. With Brenda, I could tell by the inflections in her voice when to speak and when to keep quiet. When she spoke using a baby-like voice, a higher and slower pitched whine, I knew I was safe. If her tone of voice was deep, sharp, and loud, I knew to stay out of sight, but be close enough to get to her quickly whenever she called. I also knew to how to *fix my face*, which meant keeping my face nondescript, non-threatening, and without attitude. Otherwise, I'd be met with a "You got something you want to say?" and possibly an open palm slap across the face before a command to "Fix your damn face." I did not know it then but the ability to read body language and voice inflections and to keep a nondescript face and an even voice would serve me well in adulthood when I navigated white spaces.

All days weren't bad with Brenda. She was artistic and would paint portraits of me while I sat in front of her for hours. Even though I was afraid that I wasn't still enough to keep her from fussing, she was usually so happy to be painting she didn't care. She was a seamstress and made patterns for clothing for me out of newspaper. My favorite outfit was a navy and white striped terry cloth two-piece tube top and skirt. I wore it until it pulled apart at the seams. Brenda was also a fantastic cook, a skill she said she learned in training school while growing up. When we were in the kitchen together, she would tell me training school stories of how she had to clean the bathroom floor with a toothbrush and how she placed her feet on top of a towel to mop floors. I loved watching her cook, and then eating the food she had made from scratch. She did not use anything from a box or a can, as she believed in making everything. When she made chicken and dumplings, she pin-rolled and cut the dough for dumplings. She fried chicken to perfection, and I have not had cornbread like hers since I left.

We were food stamp recipients and near the end of the month it was challenging for us to put enough things together for a delectable meal. While Brenda worked, I went outside and played with children in the neighborhood. I hoped their mothers would invite me to eat dinner with them. Most of the times I was lucky. And I always got back home before Brenda did, because she had a strict rule forbidding me to go outside the house or let people into her house when she was not at home.

One day, I was extremely hungry. I walked four apartment complexes over to visit a new friend Brenda had made, whose daughter Bonita was already in high school. Instead of waiting for them to offer food to me, I asked for it. "May I please have something to eat?" I asked, without shame. The mother did not hesitate to go into the kitchen and pull out Tupperware dishes holding last evening's meals. "Go wash your hands," she said to me, while motioning for Bonita to show me where the bathroom was. I don't remember much else, but I do know I missed night falling. When I told them that I needed to get home before my mom did, the mother would not let me leave. "It's dark out there, your momma will come get you." I cringed when she added the "And, I'mma be waiting for her, too." My mother was not the type of woman you waited for.

I was awakened by my mother's voice calling for me from outside, and by its slow, clumsy speech pattern I knew she had been drinking. Bonita's mother answered the door, and I heard her calmly talking to Brenda, asking if I could spend the night since I was already asleep. I knew spending the night in someone else's house would not happen.

Bonita and I sat up straight in her bed. I asked her to pray with me. Bonita had already put her hands in mine before I could get out the full request. We squeezed each other's hands, as it was clear Bonita was not used to such cussing and fussing, and I feared that her mom was going to be dragged out of her house. Brenda was adamant about not letting me spend the night with people if they weren't family. I can only imagine how fiercely she might have wanted to protect me since I had already been raped at four years old and she had no idea who the perpetrator was. The combination of fear, thinking I might be sexually assaulted again or that she would lose me again, mixed with anger at me for breaking the rules was probably too much, and I knew that she was not going to let me spend the night, no matter how much Bonita's mother pleaded. I tuned the argument out so I could pray.

Brenda had become more belligerent, so I got up out of bed to get dressed. "I'm going to just go home with her, so y'all can get some rest," I told Bonita. By the time I got dressed and was headed out of the bedroom, I heard Brenda say something like, "First damn thing in the morning." And her voice got distant and more distant, as I realized she was leaving and that a miracle had just occurred.

Bonita and her mother were still asleep when I found a Southern Bell telephone book. I don't know how I knew to look in the blue pages in the middle of the monstrous book to find the phone number listed for child abuse and neglect. I tensed up when I heard a male's voice on the other end of the phone.

He greeted me hello twice, because I couldn't answer the first time. "Yes," I said, trying to sound adult-like. "I have a friend who is being abused by her mom and she needs help." The man asked me to explain how I knew the friend was being abused, and if I had seen any bruises on her. "Yes, she's got burns on her arms and legs. She has bruises too and I've seen her with nose bleeds where her mom hit her in the face. Is there anything you can do to help her?" The voice on the other end asked, "You seem to know a lot about this friend. How do you know so much?" He was wasting time with these dumb questions, and I needed to get home before Brenda woke up. "We are best friends. She tells me everything." It crushed me when he said, "Well, I don't know if I can help her. I'd have to see her myself. Where is she?" the man asked. I broke down in tears, sobbing loudly and uncontrollably, awakening Bonita. I held the bottom end of the phone close to my lips and said, "I am the friend." Bonita went and got her mother, and they ended the call by giving the man their home address. It seemed to take forever for that white social worker car with the blue county logo on it, that I knew well, to arrive.

I was disappointed that the two social workers, a Black male and white woman, entered Bonita's home armed with nothing more to protect themselves than a polaroid camera and clipboard, should my mother arrive. Luckily, their screening process was quick, long enough for them to take photos of the burns and bruises on my legs and arms left by steam irons, curling irons, and other household items. The car ride to Aunt Lorraine and Uncle Charles' house was a full 10 minutes of agonizing fright and worry that went away after three weeks of hearing no word from Brenda.

Being smart had saved my life. And I figured there was nothing wrong with being the Smart One, since I couldn't be the Pretty One. Things were fine until middle school where prettiness trumped intelligence. I'm sure I was funny-looking, but if only I had known that most middle schoolers were, I may have cut myself some slack. My skin was coffee-without-cream dark, and I was super thin with big eyes, long legs, and no butt. It might sound stupid now, but I was humiliated to be the only girl at school who was passed over when boys considered which girls' butts they would palm. I could be in a crowd with three other girls and all of them would turn around and yell, "Quit feeling my butt" to a group of boys who had snuck up behind us and covered their derrieres with the palms of their hands. I could not relate to their pain, or the satisfied smiles the girls wore. So, when I added good looks, big butt, and fair skin to the list of things I did not have I just stopped striving academically. By eighth grade I'd become the class clown. I believe that was the same grade when Brother Ali gave up too.

By the time I got to high school, I didn't need to be pretty. I was funny and I learned to use my intelligence in other ways, like how to skip school and not get caught. If my hair wasn't right or I couldn't find the right outfit, I just didn't go to school. Instead, I read books and listened to my favorite artists on cassette tapes and wrote down the lyrics. When I did go to school, I could be found in the middle of the hallway leading a quartet I'd formed, impersonating gospel artists. Our peers would gather around us and encourage us because we'd learned to sound just like Maggie Ingram and the Ingramettes, Mahalia Jackson, and Willie Banks and the Messengers. Looking back, I see that my father used his influence to lead a group of friends on successful crime sprees, and I too was leading but getting into safer trouble.

By tenth grade, I had no idea what I was supposed to be doing in school. I remember being in a large assembly where students completed registration cards for courses to take the following semester. I was so lost I simply copied off the paper of the person seated next to me. Tracey, a Black classmate of mine, told me she was registering for a French class because she planned to go to college. Until that moment, I had never engaged in a conversation with anyone about college. Tracey spoke with such confidence and resolution that I asked to see her card when she was done, and I copied it line by line. The next year, we were in the same classes, and I returned to my former studious self to keep up with her. I did everything she did. When she met with her guidance counselor, I met with mine. When she registered for and took the SAT, I did too. When Tracey applied to colleges, so did I. When Tracey received acceptance letters, mine started arriving in the mail too.

Tracey chose to go to a prestigious out-of-state university. I had applied to and was accepted into three in-state universities: Johnson C. Smith University, a historically Black college and university (HBCU) less than ten miles from my home; Winston-Salem State University, another HBCU but an hour away from home; and Appalachian State University, a predominantly white institution that I learned about when its Black student gospel choir performed at my church. It was two hours away. I had three great choices and a history of making poor decisions. I was scared out of my mind to decide what direction I should turn my future life toward and ended up using distance as my compass. ASU was the furthest away and I had an inherent pain and a biological mother I needed to outrun. I knew neither of them would follow me to the mountains. I also knew there was a whole world out there I didn't know but I was determined to find out how white people lived because one day I was going to live among them.

CHAPTER 2

Where the White People Live

*T*he first time I realized that God might have lived in a place other than my heart was when I arrived in Boone, North Carolina for college. At 3333 feet in the air, God's could-be home was nestled in a valley of the Blue Ridge Mountains, namely Appalachian State University. The place I nicknamed *Heaven* was made up of statuesque brick buildings spread across 400 acres of forest green grass, the tallest trees, and beautiful flowers of various hues. Its beauty was punctuated by ponds, hills, and tunnels, with a backdrop of majestic mountains. Its crisp air enabled me to exhale more fully than I'd ever been able to do in my childhood.

I'd never felt so safe. And to keep it that way I buried my past as deep as I could in the basement of my mind. Having been adopted for the second time, by my Aunt Lorraine and Uncle Charles about five years before college, I knew that safety wasn't as big an issue to me as belonging. Being one of 300 Black students out of the 8000 Appalachian Mountaineers challenged my sense of belonging. For starters, my freshman roommate called me two days after check-in to tell me we wouldn't be rooming together. Her parents didn't think it was a good idea for her to live with a Black person. Interestingly, instead of me knowing it was their loss, I somehow believed the loss was mine, evidence that assimilation had already begun.

Then, on the first day of my communications course, where I believed I would be trained to become a TV journalist, the professor told us that his class was comprised of two kinds of students. "You're either stars or bullshitters," he exclaimed from in front of the lecture-style classroom. "And you'll know which one you are by your grade on the first exam. Stars will make above a C, and any grade lesser will belong to bullshitters." I made a D.

If I had the social capital my white counterparts had, I would have known that the failure belonged to the professor and not me. He had erroneously divided his class up into two categories based on his own culture or ethnicity as a frame of reference to judge us without considering the social and cultural factors that make us unique. Perhaps among the majority of his students—with their second- and third-generation pedigree—there were stars and bullshitters. But, he had not taken into account that at least one of the students who sat before him was a first-generational who was smart but had no study skills. Who unlike the students he was used to teaching did not know how to ask for help, or even knew that I needed it. I took responsibility for the bullshit and immediately changed my major to psychology. Studying how to undo bullshit-ism was more of a natural choice than going to counseling. Telling people my problems was not something I was raised to do, especially not to white people.

Psychology came easily to me. Even with so many theorists,

theories, and terms to describe behaviors, I was able to remember them all by ascribing them to family members who had similar features and characteristics. To understand agoraphobia, I thought of one of my late relatives who rarely stepped foot outside and stopped at the threshold of the door as if it was an invisible fence. I had a handful of family members whose behaviors helped me understand bipolar disorder, as I recalled times they were super energetic and engaging in self-seeking risks as well as times when they were at their absolute lowest. To understand panic attacks, I thought about family members whose "bad nerves" would flare up on the first of the month when bills were due, or when people made too-sudden movements or loud noises, and when crowds got too big for comfort. There were too many relatives whose lack of regard for authority and long arrest records helped me understand conduct disorder and antisocial personality disorder, among the children and adults. Knowing that apples don't fall too far from the tree, I was able to use myself as a case study for remembering the symptoms for post-traumatic stress disorder, reactive attachment disorder, body dysmorphic disorder, and several of the sexual disorders, because I met the criteria.

I thought I'd found the cure for bullshitting while studying child psychology because I was doing well. I made As and Bs in my courses and worked as a student research assistant to a prolific psychology professor. But one day I was in my room studying when the Oprah Winfrey show came on the television. It was just background noise, and I was half-attentive until I looked up and noticed a young Black girl sitting on Oprah's couch. I turned the volume up and listened to this brave soul with pigtails—I swear she looked no older than seven or eight—tell her story about being molested. I came undone, slid off the bed and onto the floor where there was more room for me to rock back and forth and to and fro, trying to ease the tension I felt in my entire body. That episode tore me apart and I was not okay. I struggled to catch my breath, I couldn't stop the tears from falling from my eyes, my heart felt as if it would punch its way out of my chest, and the guttural sounds coming from the depths of my soul scared me even the more. I had never reacted in such a way, and couldn't believe that all of that came about just from hearing this little girl on television telling my story. I tried holding myself together by pinning my knees to my chest with a vice grip and when that provided no relief I knew I needed help. Without calling for an appointment, I made my way across campus to the student counseling center, hoping to find someone who could be there for me the way Oprah was there for that little girl.

The center accepted me as a walk-in client, and I met with an older white woman counselor. She patiently listened to me recount my triune of trauma, which up to that point had been the three biggest negative and critical incidents of my life: sexual assaults, adoptions, and physical abuse. There was so much more to tell but by her struggle to find the words to reflect or summarize our session I knew I had overwhelmed her in just one hour. I also knew she was not the right counselor for me when she prescribed inner child work. "The four-year-old in you is strong and resilient. She needs to be loved and nurtured. Would you like to get in touch with her?" To me, this was some white people stuff and a reminder of why Black people like me keep things to ourselves. Her recommendation was too esoteric for me. She had made it sound as if we could call the child up on a phone and talk to her. "Heck no. I've seen enough little girls for one day. The one on Oprah about did me in. No thank you." Without even knowing what the counselor would lead me to do, I knew reconnecting with my four-year-old self would be re-traumatizing for me. There was nothing I could think of that we'd talk about—I had no memories of her playing, laughing, or enjoying life. I only remembered watching myself from above, seeing her lying sprawled out across my maternal grandmother's quilted bed, with Brenda and her sister on both sides of me trying to figure out why I was so listless and feverish. I didn't want to talk to her about that, so I didn't return for a second session. Instead, I chose to make good on the hope I had as a four-year-old patient who wanted to live as joyfully as those white candy stripers who volunteered at the hospital. So in addition to studying my family and myself through psychology, I began studying how white people lived.

The first thing I learned is that white people spoke differently from me and the people I knew. When I raised my hand in class to ask or answer questions, I said things like, "I done did that already," "Why is you bringing that up?," "I be tired of reading about Freud," and "I looked-ed real good when I had on that dress." Like the people I knew, I pronounced street and strawberry as *skreet* and *skrawberry*, and store and four as *stoe* and *foe*. At first, I didn't recognize that peers who "piggybacked" on what I'd said were rephrasing my sentences in their responses. Then, I noticed that professors did the same thing and I realized they were indirectly correcting me. Being born under the Leo sun, I have a personality that hates to look incompetent so I grew my vocabulary by looking up the words they used in the dictionary, and I practiced using them in sentences. I also learned that I was mispronouncing several words such as ambulance, salmon, specific, ask, and so on. I did not know *conversate* was not a word. I only knew that my lexicon was growing when I spoke to family and friends. One time I called home and asked Momma Lorraine to send a *photograph* of me as a child for a class assignment. She retorted, "Photograph? You mean picture?" On another occasion, I called to tell her that I had learned something about the *rap artist* Tupac, and with a laugh she asked, "Rapper?" I didn't dare use the more scholarly language I was learning because I didn't want my family to think I was trying to be better than them.

I became adept at code-switching—tailoring my speech and behavior to the occasion. Even now, when I go home, I speak my family's language, African American Vernacular English, or AAVE, or more commonly known as Ebonics. "Momma, whatchu cooking today?" I might ask. Or I'll say, "I'mma buy dat when I get the money" or "What had happened..." Additionally, I speak with slang—informal words and phrases—that someone outside the community may not know. I can easily be heard saying, "That's what's up," even though I am not talking about direction. "It's all good," I might say to let someone know that I approve, or that I've forgiven an indiscretion, or you might hear it after I've experienced something disappointing and may not be ready to be honest about how I feel about it. "You acting stank" has nothing to do with a person's body odor, but it means someone has a sour attitude. The way some Black people enunciate words, put them together, slow down or speed up the cadence, or choose words to describe something is *everything* to me. But doing so was frowned on in the white spaces I was navigating, and, like white folks correcting me, I began correcting other Black folks. I thought I was helping Black people out by teaching them the correct way to say things, but thinking that Black people need help, or that the collective language is wrong, and handing them the white standards I had grasped was not help, it was oppressive and a derivative of internalized racism.

I had not even heard of internalized racism before I got into a doctoral program in my early 40s but had been living with it for over 20 years since I began matriculating through the academic programs of Appalachian State. My simple interpretation of internalized racism is when a person of color believes and endorses white lies about their own people. It is hard not to do so when the news and media outlets perpetuate white superiority and such lies like Black people are dangerous, that we clog up the welfare system, that we are lazy and produce half-assed work, that we are not beautiful and that our children are bad. Internalized racism means that white women weren't the only ones clutching their purses when a Black person approached them, I did too. White people weren't the only ones presuming that Black women with non-traditionally colored hair and nails were ignorant and ghetto, I did too as I made sure my hair was straight and dyed black and only my got French manicures and pedicures. White people weren't the only ones shaking their heads at Black people who pronounced the letter r as a multisyllabic word.

I also did not know that hating things about Black people was a direct reflection of my own self-hatred that I projected onto other Black people. It was mind-blowing to me when I eventually realized that I did not love myself. I couldn't have been convinced that I did not love myself; to me, the evidence of my love was put into a creating a better life for myself. But, now it makes total sense. To look at another person who looks like me and think they are dangerous, ignorant, unlovable, and so on means I also believe the same about myself. Thus, the gateway to assimilation.

During the process of assimilation, my vernacular wasn't the only thing that changed. During one of my visits back home, my childhood best friend asked me, "Since when you start dressing like a white girl?" That was such an odd question, so I asked her to explain how white girls dressed. She simply pointed to my outfit and said, "Like that." I looked down at myself and saw the white Liz Claiborne button-down shirt rolled up to my forearms, the white Banana Republic ankle-length pants, and Birkenstocks on my feet and immediately understood how she came to that conclusion. Then, like a good prosecutor she rested her case, "And you know Black people don't wear Jesus shoes."

I looked at my friend's outfit and just a year before that time we would have been dressed similarly, if not identically, since we wore each other's clothes. Our wardrobe had included jeans of various colors and solid-colored shirts purchased at the mall from CitiTrends and Rainbow. Our shoes and purses had come from Pay Less. But in such a short time, my closet and dresser drawers housed Duckhead shorts, patterned blouses, blue and black pairs of Levi's jeans, and anything from Ann Taylor, Gap, and Express. I swear I owned every color of those flat ballet-looking Sam & Libby shoes. I don't remember intentionally changing my style of dress. No one had told me that the way I dressed was off, too urban, or not good enough, nor had they instructed me on what to wear. I simply took notes from my white classmates' dress and followed suit.

The biggest contributor to my dress change was having new-found access to credit cards and department store catalogs, and not having a car. I received cards and catalogs in my university post office box and discovered shopping via mail. I fell in love with stores I'd never heard of—J. Crew, Express, and New York & Company. Whenever I rode the university's shuttle bus to the mall to find these stores, I was introduced to other stores like them. In my defense if one is needed, there were no urban clothing stores in Boone. In fact, there was nothing urban about Boone at all. There were no Black hairstylists, except for one and when he applied relaxer creme to my scalp and brushed it with a hairbrush I knew he was a Black hairstylist but not a hairstylist for Black people. There were no products for Black hair in the stores—no hair grease or oil conditioners, no boar bristle brushes, or gels. I couldn't even find a Black-centric magazine on the store shelves and no matter how many white women magazines I bought, nothing felt like a salve to my soul like the *Essence* magazine I subscribed to. I remember the celebration we had when after many student requests Appalachian State subscribed to Black Entertainment Television (BET). It was a joy to get dressed for morning classes with my favorite music videos playing in the background. Boone was white-white, which meant I hit the jackpot for trying to learn a different lifestyle.

My music was probably already all over the place; MTV and VH-1 in the late 80s brought white music into our home. My family loved R&B, rap, blues, and gospel—all things BET. But the two aforementioned music television stations had us also loving Talking Heads, the Eurythmics, Van Halen, and Bruce Springsteen. Even deeper, at Appalachian State we listened to Garth Brooks, Eric Clapton, Bonnie Raitt, Red Hot Chili Peppers, Guns N' Roses, and Nirvana, just to name a few artists. My music choices grew even whiter roots when I ended up with a Black roommate who liked The Doors, The Carpenters, and Loretta Lynn and I learned to love their albums too.

Appalachian State was aptly known as Happy Appy. It felt like one big love fest—white and Black people fellowshipping together at parties, on the lawn, in the tunnels, at the games, and in its cafeterias. It was my first experience with racial colorblindness. It was common to hear folks say that the human race was the only race we needed to concern ourselves with. We'd come to believe things like "we put our pants on the same way, we bleed the same color blood, there is no difference between us." Most of the professors were warm. It was my white woman English professor who gave me her personal copy of Gloria Naylor's *Mama Day* and held discussions with me about it. That was impactful to me for quite a few different reasons—I would have never pegged her as a reader of Black literature, and her excitement about the book was contagious so I felt compelled to read it even though I didn't see the purpose of reading for fun when I had a desk full of textbooks to get through. Moreover, the fact that she gave me her personal copy was noteworthy because any book lover has a first rule to never give or loan personal copies of our books. Mostly, this exchange was important to me because one of the main characters was an orphan who had to suspend his beliefs to accept the otherworldliness of his new wife's home of origins. This professor and I had never had a conversation about my upbringing but that character's story resonated with me, with Appalachian State being my otherworldly place where I lost footing on the Blackness I had been rooted and grounded in.

Happy Appy was full of basically three kinds of white people. There were the hippies who were affectionately called "tree-huggers" or "granolas." These students were "natural," and dressed in free-flowing clothing and Jesus-shoes, ate vegan or vegetarian, and were super laid back. Then, there were the students who could be found sunbathing or playing hacky sack in the yard with their leashed ferrets nearby. I had never seen or heard of a ferret until App, and I haven't seen one since I left. Lastly, there were the cool white students who wanted to be where the Black students were. They could easily be found listening and dancing to Dr. Dre and Snoop with us. A few of the bolder ones took up our causes, and some pledged Black sororities and fraternities. And when their parents came to visit them, they made sure to see us too. Just as my parents did when they visited me.

Another dynamic that contributed to the Happy Appy effect was communal giving. Even though I was a broke college student, there were only a few times I needed money and couldn't readily access it. Whoever had money gave it freely. I didn't have to buy food or alcohol. If I needed a ride, there was always someone willing to drive or loan me their car. In fact, I owe my very first beach trip to my college friends. I had never been to the beach, had no idea what it was, besides sand and water, and I couldn't grasp what that might look like or why anybody would want to go there. We piled up as many friends as we could into three cars and headed toward Myrtle Beach, South Carolina. I felt super vulnerable going somewhere without money or my family to depend on. I learned to trust people outside of my family at Happy Appy.

As one beginning to lose my racial identity I did not recognize that App's communal nature was not that different from the collective nature of the communities I grew up in. Whether it was the subsidized housing projects I grew up in while under Brenda's care where it was common for neighbors to borrow a cup of sugar or flour or a couple of cigarettes, or to use someone's house phone; or the residential community Momma Lorraine and Daddy Charles raised me in. I do not recall much borrowing of goods in our neighborhood but what I fondly remember was the collective child rearing. Adults along our street watched out for one another's houses, children, and families. Once, I skipped school and a neighbor down the street scolded me and then called Momma Lorraine to tell her I was at home. People looked out for one another. I am convinced that when we lived in neighborhoods we were neighbors, but when we moved into subdivisions we became divided.

But I do not have any room to judge any one because I left the neighborhood on the first train smoking, in search of a better life. I wish I could have talked to my family about the changes going on with me but I did not have the language or the words to articulate my experiences, and we weren't the kind of family that talked about deep or painful things. Having been adopted, I spoke very little about anything that might have made my family think I was not appreciative of them and what they did for me. I know my family noticed, though, because there was a Black family who lived across the street from us and we joked about them acting white. Looking back, I am not sure why we thought they were acting anything other than Black. They dressed nicely, spoke properly, drove nice cars, and kept to themselves. They were always the first on the street to get the newest things—a microwave, VCR, the Atari, an above-ground pool in the backyard, and a computer. Their children were the first on our street to go to college. Although we thought that they thought they were better than everybody else, I secretly admired them. Today's young folks would call them Black excellence.

I was in my last semester of undergraduate school and making plans to go back home when I received what came to be a life-changing letter in my post office box. The letter was an invitation to apply to App State's master's degree in counseling program. I had never even heard of a master's degree when the letter from Dr. Leroy Baruth, the chair of the program, reached me. I wasted no time going over to the department to find this Black man because I didn't know there was another faculty member of color on campus. I looked forward to asking him a few questions. First, I wanted to know why he thought I'd make a good candidate; my Grade Point Average wasn't even a 3.0. I also wanted to ask him what a master's degree was, what it would permit me to do, how much it would cost me, and how long it would take me to complete. I sat in the lobby waiting for him to come get me when a white man approached me and confirmed my name. Heck, I confirmed his name because I had never known a white man named Leroy and haven't met one since.

Dr. Baruth was a gentle man, and he patiently answered my questions. He encouraged me to take the GRE (Graduate Record Examinations) test, even though I told him I doubted I could pass it. "I have confidence in you, LaTonya. I look forward to hearing your good news after you pass the exam." He invited me back to his office any time. On the way of out the door, he confided, "My goal is to diversify the counseling department, which in turn would diversify the counseling profession. I believe you can help me do it."

I left his office bewildered, as I had not had much interaction with white men, and I'd never met one who believed I could help him do something. His approach was very different from the star-versus-bullshitter professor I had in my first semester, and I left his office believing in myself and knowing I would help advance his mission. I bought the GRE study book and scheduled the exam for four weeks' time. I passed the exam by one point! Dr. Baruth was the first person I called to tell him the good news and I don't know who was more excited—him or me.

I was only the Black student in my cohort but that did not bother me as much as it could or should have. By this point, I had already started losing myself and my Blackness. I do not recall any racial incidents, or racial microaggressions but that does not mean that there were not any. It just means that I was so racially colorblind that I did not perceive the wrongdoings. When one assimilates, they assume faults rather than putting responsibility on the perpetuator. Plus painful things kept happening in my family life that made me not want to look back. One time, I couldn't find a ride home for Thanksgiving break during my first semester in graduate school. For whatever reason, my parents did not come to get me. I cannot remember if they did not come because I did not ask them or because they couldn't. Either way, I was forced to stay in my apartment with very little food and money and the campus was shut down. No matter how far I thought I'd gotten away from my childhood, it often felt like it was on my heels. Somehow, Dr. Baruth heard that I was staying behind and invited me to have dinner with his family. That was the first time I had set foot inside a white person's home (well, the second if I count the foster home experiences). The four-year-old inside me felt abandoned, having been left stranded in Boone, but it was counterbalanced by the excitement of having a semblance of proof that I was doing what I set out to do—to have been so accepted by white people that I was welcomed into their home.

I learned so much at that dinner table—first, white people's cuisine was different (no, there were no peanut butter and syrup sandwiches). I was already a picky eater, with a palate for McDonald's, Taco Bell, and southern cuisine when I was at home. So, I helped myself to a spoonful of foods I'd never had—green bean casserole, sweet potatoes with marshmallows, macaroni and cheese topped with breadcrumbs, and a slice of roasted turkey with sprigs of parsley and kale as garnishment. I wasn't familiar with the taste of pecan or meringue pies either but I didn't eat those. I was also used to drinking sweeter iced tea. My plate was less full than it would have been at home where my family was sure to be eating a sugar-cured ham and a roasted spice-injected turkey, candied yams, collard greens cooked with pork, potato salad, rice and gravy, pinto beans, blackberry cobblers, apple pie with ice cream, and pound cake. All but the chitterlings would have lined my plate. The table was quieter at the Baruths' house than at home too, and I remember feeling super nervous; my body temperature was higher than their thermostat and I knew it wasn't from the abundant warmth of their hospitality. I was too busy hoping

I sounded as smart as my hosts. I sat up straighter, I thought about what I said before I said it, and I followed their cues to know when to speak, laugh, and finish my dinner. Because our communication styles and senses of humor were different, these things weren't easy for me to discern.

I didn't think I was acting white at that table, or any time afterwards. I simply thought I was learning and doing what I needed to give myself an advantage. I believed I should be able to have access to everything white people had. I should have access to a good education, safe lodging, and money. If speaking properly, dressing differently, showing up on time, and developing a sense of dry humor were my ticket to those things then I just took it as a compliment when my Black counterparts said I was acting white, and when white people told me I was different from other Black people. I had no idea I was in too deep and that the stakes would get higher.

CHAPTER 3
Black Girl Magic

*A*s an ice-breaker, my new sixth-grade homeroom teacher asked the class to name a superpower we wished we had. My peers giggled as they raised their hands and called out heroic abilities like flying, being bionic, leaping over buildings, running really fast, shape shifting, and lassoing bad guys. I considered all those things too, but by the time I'd got to that class—my third sixth-grade classroom in one academic year—I was exhausted from fear. The ink hadn't yet dried on my adoption papers and I was afraid to trust the process.

Imagining a superpower might have been a game to my homeroom peers, but it was a prayer for me. After enduring bouts of childhood homelessness, neglect, and physical and sexual abuse, I prayed for the superpower to be invisible. I surmised that I couldn't be hurt if I couldn't be seen.

And God answered me, too. The boys passing me over in middle and high school was evidence of my invisibility. I watched on the sidelines as my peers' boyfriends carried their books and walked them to their classes. I celebrated with my friends when treats and balloons were delivered to class from boyfriends and secret admirers on Valentine's Day. I was not surprised or bummed when I was not invited to the school dances or the junior and senior prom.

By that time, I'd also become invisible inside the classroom. I was tired of being smart, and when I acted like the class clown, teachers mustered the strength to ignore and overlook my smart mouth. I was not even on the guidance counselor's radar as one to go to college. There was not an athletic bone in my body, so I didn't play sports, and I didn't have the talent or courage to try theater, chorus, or any of the clubs that might have made me more visible.

Even if I was not invisible at home, I did my best to stay out of the way. Aunt Lorraine and her husband Charles adopted me from foster care when I was 12 years old. By that time, their daughter Luck was nine and they had a preschool-aged son, whom we nicknamed Chuck. Our home life was stable, family-centered, and it did not take me too long to transition to regarding my aunt, uncle, and cousins as mom, dad, and my siblings. My parents worked and served traditional family roles—with Dad being the provider and protector and Mom being the nurturer. Momma Lorraine was more of the disciplinarian, and we all got our share of whippings. Those whippings were nothing compared to Brenda's "excessive discipline" as the child court called it. Luck was an unruly teenager and there were times when Daddy Charles had to intervene. The most he ever disciplined me was through lectures that lasted one to two hours. I appreciate the stern talking-tos now, but then I would rather have been given a one- or two-minute whipping and been done with discipline.

Life was positively different there. I had access to food—the pantry, refrigerator, and freezer were always stocked. There were always toiletries. We did not move from house to house. We always had a car. My parents were always employed (until Luck had her first baby, and Momma Lorraine quit her job because she wanted to be a full-time grandmother). I did not have to cook, clean, or iron my parents' clothes as I was used to. They took care of us and did not need me to take care of them. I did not have to wash clothes by hand in the tub and hang them up to dry on the clothesline. They threw birthday parties for us, and we got Christmas gifts. They were present, and when they were not at home, they told us where they were going and when they would return. They were dependable and trustworthy. We got allowances. They supported our goals—one time Luck and I wanted our own candy store so they bought everything we needed and let us sell cups of frozen Kool-Aid, candy, dill pickles, and whatever else we could think of. We set up shop in our front yard for two summers straight.

Although the differences were positive, I struggled with them. Brenda had made decisions for me, but Momma Lorraine and Daddy Charles let me choose for myself, even when I chose nothing. I was a thorn in Lorraine's side when she asked what I wanted to eat, what movie I wanted to watch, or which pair of shoes I liked. Because I was afraid of being a burden, or choosing something too costly, or messing up, making decisions felt like torment to me. It felt strange going from being super responsible as a parentified child to only being responsible for doing well in school, so I did things Luck and Chuck did not do. I kept our yard tidy by sweeping the porch and walkway. Our house was on the corner, so I picked up trash left by passers-by. More strangely, I washed the vinyl siding on our house when it got dirty. I got my first job when I was 15 and purchased my own clothing, shoes, and hair products. Within months, I'd saved enough money to purchase my first car with the help of a neighbor. Looking back, I realize I did way too much. But since my parents never said anything about my overworking and didn't try to stop me, their silence endorsed my feelings of invisibility. Perhaps, I was trying to be seen.

Recently, my new therapist asked me what things my mother (Lorraine) and I did together. I could not remember any. She asked if we had mother–daughter dates, if we went shopping for my prom dress together, or if my mother was by my side when I gave birth to my children. The answer was no to all those questions. I'd always excused her from those things because she had two other children to raise and be there for. The therapist thought that was odd, and that I was overly content being an invisible child.

I was invisible for my first semester of college. I stayed in my room mostly, only going out to go to class or get food. I socialized with a few of the girls on my hall. After the Christmas break, I got a last-minute roommate, a Black girl named Charli. Charli was everything I was not. She was sophisticated in dress, and regal in the way she carried herself. Even her name was badass and she drove a blue Jeep Wrangler. Charli took up space wherever she went. She never played small and was not afraid to make her voice heard. I became popular just by being her roommate, and she made sure I looked the part. She took me to parties and introduced me to people. She nicknamed me Black, because of my dark skin, but the way it rolled off her tongue it could not be mistaken as an insult. It was the first time I'd ever heard someone celebrate darkness. Charli saw me and led me to see myself. I was no longer invisible, and I came to appreciate being seen.

By my sophomore year, Charli had withdrawn from school, and I had made three best friends—Benita, Victoria, and Precious. Those fellow North Carolinians were as bold and confident as Charli. Victoria's confidence is exemplified by a comment she made one day: "I'm pretty and I ain't got no ugly friends." I looked around at the four of us and did a mental check off. Yep, Victoria was pretty with her even-toned caramel skin, full lips, and high cheekbones. Yep, Benita was pretty and could have been a model with her tall, lanky frame and beautiful face accentuated by a mane of long thick hair. Yep, Precious was pretty and her Liberian beauty was punctuated by the athlethic body she acquired being a track star. I couldn't see my beauty so much. Brenda had called me names and *ugly* was the nicest of them. Even Momma Lorraine had said I used to be an ugly duckling. The way I saw it, if my family members thought I was nothing to look at then invisibility was a favor to us all. But I challenged myself to take Victoria's word for it, because even though she wasn't a family member she didn't have a reason to lie. What an empowering decision that was. I practiced mantras to reinforce what I had been told, and I looked myself in the mirror so I could hear and observe myself say, "I am pretty." Through those women, I practiced self-love under their unconditional support, which they probably didn't recognize they were giving as they were just being themselves. We partied together, fought for one another, and stuck by each other's sides through good times, heartaches, and loss. We finished school and were separated by distance as I had stayed at Appalachian for graduate school.

I felt invisible among the men at Appalachian State. I was passing by the players of the football team at a party once when I learned I wore the scarlet letter S. One of the players said, "You're fine as hell but you're too little. You need to come eat at the training table." I picked up my pace and quickly moved my size zero frame past his teammates as they laughed. On another occasion, a guy pointed out that my ankles were super small. I had never paid enough attention to people's ankles to notice any differences. All this time I thought I was overlooked because I was unattractive and dark, only to add skinny to the list.

It didn't help that most of the 300 Black students were women. The odds were in male students' favor, with them having two to three girlfriends at a time. So, the odds for finding love were stacked high against me. However, it was the 1990s and I was in love with Treach, the rapper from the group Naughty by Nature, and there was a student who, to me, was a replica. He was the same 5'10 height, same milk chocolate colored skin, and same swag—wearing baggy pants, tank tops, a baseball hat to the back, and a gold chain. Heck, he even had a machete. Now, any smart girl might have exited at the sight of such a large knife, but I came from a family of knife-wielding women who were not afraid to use them. So, I was not afraid. Plus, Brenda and Momma Lorraine had said that I was so full of book sense that I lacked common sense.

I don't remember how I made my interest known, or if my love interest was the first to flirt, but with Treach at the forefront of my mind, it felt as if I'd hit the jackpot being with him. As long as he made me feel like his number one girlfriend, I didn't care how many others he had. As long as he answered my calls, accompanied me to parties, and acknowledged me on the yard, I was willing to put up with sharing him. I gave him my virginity and stayed in his rotation of girls for a year. Then, fall break of our sophomore year came and as scheduled, I reached home four hours before he did. By evening, I was annoyed that I had not yet heard from him so when my sister Luck told me the ringing phone was for me, I was ready to fuss him out. The voice on the other line belonged to one of my college suitemates calling to let me know that my boyfriend had been in a bad accident. He had been airlifted to the trauma center after an 18-wheeler had pummeled over his burgundy IROC-Z. His close friend and passenger had already been checked in and out of the hospital but my boyfriend had been badly hurt and was in critical condition.

The phone calls from peers kept coming and it took a day or two for me to muster the courage to go and visit him. I did not want to see him as they described—unconscious, motionless, and breathing only by a machine. The four-step walk into the waiting room from the door felt longer than the ten-minute one I took from the car into the hospital to the elevator. There, I met his mother—a tall, thin figure with her grey-black hair drawn back into a ponytail, standing at the window staring down at nothing when I approached her. To her, I was no different from all the other App students who steadily came in to visit. I introduced myself and it was clear he had not mentioned me to her. After some small talk, she walked me over to her ex-husband, his stepfather, whose face was buried in a newspaper. He was much more personable, and I spent most of my time with him, while we waited on the next visiting hour. His parents let me go to see him by myself. My body shook as I walked the narrow and sterile hallway. My stomach threatened to empty the cheeseburger and small Coke I had wolfed down about an hour before. I rubbed my stomach to calm it down as I entered his room. I found him just as others had described. A nurse was attending to him, and she turned around when I got closer. The nurse told me that while he would live, he would never walk again, and they were not sure if he would even return to college. She encouraged me to talk to him, she said he could hear my voice. I did talk to him. I don't remember what I said, but if nothing else I prayed for him. I left some of the visiting time to his parents, and before I left the hospital his father said to me, "You're going to marry my son."

I left the hospital not knowing what to think about his father's assertion. On the one hand, I was flattered. Out of all the girls who'd visited—and I'd heard there were plenty—his dad saw and chose me. On the other hand, how could I marry a man who was not expected to walk or speak? I left the hospital and continued to pray for him. Months passed by before I drove to his hometown to visit him. He had self-willed his way to wellness. Despite the physician's report, he had taught himself to walk, he had listened to his body and eaten what he believed would restore his health, and although he had lost a lot of his remote memory, he remembered me. After a few years, he returned to the university. I was in graduate school by then.

Our courtship resumed, and one evening I invited him to my apartment for dinner to celebrate his return to school. He came to my apartment and in a matter-of-fact manner, as he always displayed, he asked me to marry him. There was no must, no fuss, no ring, and no romanticism. My mouth said yes but my mind screamed no. We were 22 years old and I had no idea what my future held. So, I asked for a year-long engagement. I figured we'd be broken up by then.

Plus, I needed to keep my attention on school. One of my professors had asked me and two other students to present with her at a flagship conference for our profession. The conference was going to be held in Denver, Colorado, and there was no way I was going to get there by plane. I'd never flown before and it did not make sense for me pay someone to kill me in an airplane crash. The two women students and I decided that we would make the 26-hour drive to Colorado. I was appreciative of Dr. Baruth's support—without me asking, he handed me a $500 check to get there and back. The students and I rented a minivan and loaded it up with juice boxes, beef jerky, and Lunchables. The road trip was fun, except for my many requests for bathroom stops, there and back.

As soon as we got back, I asked my neighbor and best friend Kim to go with me to the infirmary to get something for motion sickness from the drive. When I explained my symptoms—sick to the stomach, no energy, and light headedness—the nurse recommended a urine sample. A few minutes later, Dr. Dennis appeared, a kind male doctor I knew well because I was always in the infirmary for symptoms of one illness or another. I'd checked myself in for everything from AIDS, to mad cow disease, to a skin-eating disorder. They treated me kindly each time and dismissed me with instructions and strategies to lower my stress. No one bothered to tell me I was a hypochondriac, someone whose emotional symptoms manifest physically. But this time, I didn't hear anything else Dr. Dennis said after, "Congratulations, you're pregnant."

His lips were moving so I know sound was coming out of his mouth, but I only heard silence and my thoughts. What the hell? Pregnant? I thought I couldn't have kids. My parents are going to kill me. What will I do now? It literally felt as if someone had snatched a rug from underneath my feet. I did not know how to think or feel. I wondered how I would tell my boyfriend. Kim and I went to the dollar store and found a baby bib that read *I love Daddy*. Handing him that bib was how I broke the news and it was as uneventful as our engagement. When he opened the gift bag and read the bib he questioned whether the baby was his. He recounted that the doctors had told him that the high-powered medications he was on would render him impotent. I remembered that Brenda told me the doctors said I would never have children because of the trauma of the rape I endured at four years old. Yet there we were, pregnant, so I sped the engagement up. We married before our son was born and were divorced before he turned two years old. I left him and found invisibility for me and my son in a women's shelter.

As I wished, invisibility had shielded me from danger, but it had also kept me from the mental and emotional growth and maturity I needed. I found Jesus in the shelter and hid behind the Bible for many years. I spiritually bypassed trauma and the hard work it required to heal by pursuing the promises of the Bible. I named and claimed—which meant I quoted Bible scriptures aloud like personal affirmations and believed that the results were mine to have. So when the widow in 2 Kings 4 went to the prophet asking for a financial miracle and left with a profitable business plan, I believed that as a single mother my businesses could be profitable too. I also paid into the prosperity gospel—scriptures used to promote financial gain—believing that if I gave to God He would give to me, and I laid hands on myself according to scriptures for the emotional healing I needed as I climbed the ranks of being a licensed minister and a licensed mental health counselor. I obtained what I thought was evidence of recovery from my past, including a PhD.

I was remarried when I pursued and obtained my doctorate degree. I quickly learned that invisibility while teaching in academia is a detriment. To gain worth as a faculty member of color, I and my work needed to be very visible. Otherwise, I was told I might get dinged for not being collegial or a team player if I didn't show up often. So I showed up everywhere and overworked to have something to show for my time. Unfortunately, I did not know how much productivity was enough but I figured as a person of color I needed to produce twice as much as my peers. I had become very visible across the university and in the community. My work as the founder of the annual Black Mental Health Symposium increased my visibility across the country. It didn't take long for me to accept and like being seen until the day I was accosted in my driveway by a white supremacist.

The pandemic had just been declared and my husband Nathan and I hadn't yet been in our new home for a whole month. I hadn't even hung the drapes or called for a security system, although those things were on my to-do list. But, I drifted back to old thinking by believing that being in a predominantly white neighborhood was safe enough for me to take my time. I was at the stoplight when I felt a need to look in the rearview mirror to see if anybody was behind me. My car was the only one in the turning lane to arrive in the community where we lived. I took a right into the community, made a left turn, and then turned left to reach the middle of the cul de sac where our house sits. The garage opened for me when I pressed the button in the car and I pulled into my parking space. I gathered my wallet and took a glance in the rearview mirror to check my hair and makeup to make sure I didn't come home looking tired for Nathan. I forgot about what I wanted to look like as I caught glimpse of a white pick-up truck parked directly behind me. Considering we did not know anybody in the area, I figured Nathan had finally called the repair person he'd been talking about to install the French doors he wanted in our bedroom. I ignored the truck, assuming the driver would ring the door-bell like anyone else. I was headed toward the door when the driver blew his horn at me. I noticed his *Knights Templar* front plate when I approached him and made a mental note that we needed to vet repair people more strictly in Florida than we did we lived in North Carolina. He was so close to my truck that it only took a few steps to get to his window. I asked him if I could help him. "I followed you because you have a univer-sity sticker on your car. You work there?" I furrowed my brow, partly confused and partly annoyed. I answered affirmatively. He told me that he used to work there. Then he asked me, "You live here?" With full annoyance, I answered affirmatively and asked him again how I could help him. By now, anybody else would have commanded him to leave or would have run for help. But honestly, because he wasn't verbally threatening or physically aggressive, I felt like the seven-year-old girl who sat in Brenda's car trying to figure if I was in danger. So there I was in my own front yard, feeling totally powerless and violated.

I could not make sense of the man's visit. I stood frozen, keenly aware of my movements so as not to alarm him, trying to determine what I should do while he spoke about being a former police officer for 12 years, a former employee at the university until two months ago when he was fired, and living around the corner from us. I was still rooted to the spot when he backed out of my driveway, and I stiffened when he put his truck in drive toward me because he remembered something he wanted to tell me. I was out of my mind with fear and have no idea why he thought I might want to know about sweaters he used to bring to work for his university employees. I asked him for his name, and he told me and laughed as he backed up and drove away.

I was almost late for my next meeting, but I called the university's security department where he'd told me he used to work and I asked them if the man was mentally ill or if I should be concerned for my life. They affirmed the latter and told me to make a police report and a campus police report so I could be protected on campus. I did both and learned that this man was the "Grand Poobah" of his organization and had been fired for stalking and making false claims against Black students and faculty on campus. My request for a restraining order or trespassing violation was refused by the county police department. *If I were white and I told you I had been accosted by a Black man on my property, you would have given me a restraining order and you would have stopped every Black man in a white pick-up truck until you found him*, I wanted to scream, but I said nothing. I was embarrassed at having a police car in front of my house when I had not been in the neighborhood for three weeks. *There goes the neighborhood*, I imagined my white neighbors saying, as some of them watched from the cul de sac. The university issued an immediate ban from campus against their former employee and offered to escort me to and from class for as long as needed. My department, however, did something interesting. They thought it would be best to protect me by stripping my name from my office door, the entryway to our department, the electronic billboard in the building, and the department's website. There was no evidence of me anywhere and some faculty thought I'd left the university. "I thought you were gone," they'd say, walking past my office and seeing me at my desk. I was truly invisible, wiped out, doing the work of an academician without a trace of existence.

Here I was, at the pinnacle of living and working among white people. I had made it to the Ivory Tower, as academia is called. I had accomplished the thing I promised my four-year-old self I would do. Who knew the stakes were so high? As far as I was concerned, the gods of superpowers could have invisibility back.

Outside of academia, I was not bound by an office building and there was proof of my work—scholarly journal publications, national conference and keynote presentations, the founding of *Black Mental Health Today* magazine and my annual conference, the Black Mental Health Symposium. I was nick-named Black Girl Magic by my peers, colleagues, and stakeholders. I was Black Girl Magic in public, and Black Girl Tragic in private. I recently read Dr. Rheeda Walker's book, *The Unapologetic Guide to Black Mental Health*, where she wrote that over-working was a sign of self-hatred. That was proof that I could not educate my way out of my past. It was an indication that overworking for money and accolades were not synonymous with healing and health. Personifying Black Girl Magic was not healthy.

Black Girl Magic is no longer a compliment to me, it feels like entrapment. When white women make accomplishments, they are entrusted with power or seen to be powerful, but Black women presumably possess magic. Magic is an illusion, not real or believable. It is performative, has an audience, and can be purchased. People are awe-struck by magic tricks and they demand more. Power, on the other hand, is real, it changes things and people. Powerful people are respected and their benefactors give to them rather than take. Black women are powerful. I am powerful. Many of us don't even believe in magic, especially if we believe in Jesus. But then sometimes we question the realness and power of that.

CHAPTER 4

White God, Black Theology

The first time I sincerely asked God for help, I was shivering with fright in the backseat of Brenda's car as the stormy North Carolina summer sky hurled pebbles of ice at us. I wasn't afraid of the sudden darkness, or the wind that shook the trees into violent dancing over the car, or the rapid-fire sound of hail beating against its roof. No. My nine-year-old self was terrified of the raging storm sitting in the driver's seat as Brenda pounded her fist on the steering wheel and dashboard, cursing God to His face. When she ran out of four-syllable obscenities for Him she found new ones for His mother, and that's when I got scared. I'd witnessed enough altercations to know that all hell breaks loose when somebody talks about a man's mother, especially a Black man. Only a fool would risk her life to rail against Mary. So, I prayed. Not my now-I-lay-me-down-to-sleep or God-is-great-God-is-good rudimentary prayers. Oh no, I prayed that God would not electrocute us with the lightning bolts that flashed all around. I begged Him to have mercy on my mother's soul and I asked that He forgive her for cursing Him and His mother. I rocked back and forth, wringing my hands out of angst as I waited for God to do something. I closed my eyes so I wouldn't see either storm. I pleaded with God to heal whatever my mother was mad about, and soon both storms came to an abrupt stop. It was hot and muggy when we stepped outside the foggy-windowed blue Mustang. She unlocked the door to the house, humming to herself what sounded like a hymn to me.

In my earlier years, God was not a specific race or gender. To me, God was an energy. When my younger self was sad, lonely, or pained, I accessed God by closing my eyes to see a million little silvery crystal-like thingies circulating behind my eyelids. They were always there, and always moving. I didn't pray to them. Just the sheer act of observing their movement, their vastness, and their closeness was enough to comfort and ground me. I never felt alone, although Brenda left me by myself for long periods of time.

I didn't know Brenda as a reader, but she kept books in the house. At my disposal, I had dictionaries, encyclopedias, series of story books like The Hardy Boys and Nancy Drew mysteries, and two vintage anthologies of American poetry. I was in fourth grade reading Whittier, Frost, and Whitman, over and over until the hardback covers pulled away from their threaded spine. Although I had no idea what the poets were writing about, I admired the way they put the words together. I understood enough to know that they were either talking about love or death, or both. Soon, the Bible, just another book to us, found its way into our home when, not long after the storm, I met Brenda's new boyfriend, Anthony. He was the son of a preacher and I often found him reading the Bible. I asked him to interpret the passages I overheard him reading aloud.

When Anthony saw that I was interested in the Bible, he started a study for the two of us. We began at Genesis. We read line by line, even the chapters about so-and-so-begetting-so-and-so, the genealogy most readers skip from boredom. Brenda was happy to see that her boyfriend and I got along so well. She may have felt as if she'd hit the jackpot when he brought gifts home for me after his day's work at the bread factory. I loved being thought of, and since I didn't have a lot of toys I appreciated the game of jacks, paddle balls, and the dolls he gave me.

We moved out of the house where the storm had raged and into a subsidized housing complex about a 20-minute walk away. Thankfully, I did not have to change schools. At the new place, Anthony became a jogger. He left the house for jogs around the city. I thought it was cool that he had something to do outside work, outside the house. Outside school, I had nothing else. Brenda wasn't a homebody. She always had something to do. I was able to distinguish her whereabouts by her clothing—the black dress and white chiffon apron I kept clean and ironed, with tights and black nursing shoes, meant she was going to work at an uptown hotel as a hospitality staff person. Anything brightly colored, lacey, leather, short, or tight meant she was going "out." I loved watching her get ready for either place. The care she took applying her makeup, adhering eyelashes, curling her hair, or putting her wigs on just right was so feminine, soft, and beautiful to me—and such a contrast to who she usually was, which was hard, strong, coarse-mouthed, and angry.

The beatings stopped while she had a live-in boyfriend, and I began jogging with him. It was cool to be outside, to experience transportation on foot with no destination, and by chance see my classmates out playing at the park or apartments where I didn't know they lived. One morning, Anthony challenged me to a longer jog. He said he wanted to check on the house where we had moved from. He playfully changed his mind, saying it would be too long a trek for me. Being the Leo I am—one that never backs down from a challenge—I bet him I could not only complete the jog, but I could keep up with him the entire way.

The jog to the house was fun, but opening the door to such a dark, cold, and abandoned place was anticlimactic. Some of our furnishings were still there, and it looked as if we had left in haste. I was at school when they packed up and moved. They left the dusty, tattered green couch I used to sleep on in the middle of the living room floor. I followed behind Anthony as he inspected the place, wondering exactly what he was looking for or looking at. We passed by the few dishes in the kitchen sink, then we stood still in the bedroom where he and Brenda used to sleep. The nightstand and dresser were still there and I wondered why we had come. Anthony decided we should have a quick Bible study, which was fine by me because that place felt god-forbidden. He picked me up and placed me on a dresser, and we were nearly face-to-face. He didn't have a Bible, but he said we knew enough of the passages that we didn't need it. And he was right, because as he spoke about Ham seeing his father Abraham naked and drunk, I knew exactly what he was talking about. What I didn't understand was why he was standing between my legs. I let my eyes focus on the digital alarm clock across the room where I watched the plastic black and white minute numbers fall one after the other while he assured me that he was doing nothing wrong.

The jog back home was slow. We seemed to move past

houses, cars, and people in slow motion. Anthony waved at my classmate Kissy, who was sitting in the same spot on her porch as she was when we passed her the first time. I didn't wave. My arm, legs, and heart were too heavy. Plus, I felt different, and it seemed like everyone could see what had happened to me. I felt the scarlet letter he imparted to me burning in my chest. I kept jogging. I needed to see my mother. I silently rehearsed the words I'd use to tell her, while I ignored his jokes—mere attempts to cheer me up. *Momma, he touched my private parts.*

Brenda wasn't at the house when we got there. Even when she returned, it wasn't long enough for me to make my thick tongue cooperate with the heavy words in my head. The few times that I was alone with her, he would arrive from work or the store with another gift and she'd say, "He's so good to you." Since I couldn't talk to my mother, I sought God. I figured I'd find more than the energy behind my eyelids in the Black-congregant Baptist church across the street from the housing project. By myself on the next Sunday morning, I crossed the four-lane street to get to salvation. I joined the church, walking my ten-year old self to the altar to "give my life to the Lord." I didn't know what that meant, but I hoped that the outstretched arms of the stained-glass image of a white man with cascading brunette hair and brown eyes would be enough to take away Brenda's boyfriend's impartation.

It was not odd to me that a Black church worshiped a white God. My reality was that when my family needed something, white people were the ones who granted or denied the request. The folks at the food stamp office, or the ones at the "government cheese" lines distributing free bags of food, in the hospital emergency rooms, or the principals of schools, the man in the rent office, the convenience-slash-grocery-store where we bought groceries, the police who came to the house, and finally the social workers who delivered me from hell—everywhere we turned the people who had the power to make change were white. When the preacher said that God had "all power," that sealed the deal for me.

Unfortunately, I did not know any Black people with power who could have challenged my conceptualization of all-powerful white people. The Black men I knew, like my uncles, Brenda's brothers, had "street credit," which was power of a sort. It kept them alive, but not out of trouble. My father was already serving his first ten-year prison stint for robbing banks. Brenda seemed to have more power in her relationships than the men she dated. Usually, they moved in with us and after a few fights where they'd often get beaten, they'd move out. There was only one of her boyfriends that I can remember who moved us into his home. But, we left running for our lives in the middle of the night after one of their altercations. So, no, I would never have thought of Jesus as a Black man, or a Black person.

It would take a tremendous amount of psychological effort to combat the many movies, books, and images in churches to see God as a Black man. Plus, there was no way I could believe that a Black Jesus would permit me to endure so much pain at the hands of Black people, or white people for that matter. But I was fully persuaded that a white God would.

My church attendance as a youngster was spotty. Brenda was not a church-goer. I'd get in a seasonal stint of Sunday services with Momma Lorraine. But, eventually the pains of adulthood led me back to church for myself and I did not miss a Sunday of service. To me, church was like a vaccination, it built up my immunity against the troubles of the week. I took copious notes from the preacher's sermons, and I came to believe that the word was my weapon. The preacher taught me that with Jesus I could have an abundant life, that I could do all things through Christ, and that nothing was impossible for God. I had never heard such promises and by then I had three children and I needed an abundance of possibilities for them. I needed their childhoods to be better than mine. I followed the scriptures to the tee, only listened to gospel music, and I practiced celibacy. I did not know then that I was working for God's approval as hard as I had worked for Brenda's or Momma Lorraine's.

When I wasn't in church, I watched preachers on television. Although the televangelists were different from my pastor—mostly they were white—I was intrigued by the way they used the scriptures. My pastor preached sermons from the Bible to help us manage the struggles of life. For instance, he might have preached the return of the prodigal son to encourage parents whose children were "out in the streets" to have faith that God could bring their children home. Or, he might have taught us to exercise our faith more like the woman with the issue of the blood so our prayers and desires would reach Jesus. I was in a church where we had the holy ghost but didn't have any money. That didn't make any sense to me so I began to rely on the televangelists who spoke about my biggest challenge—poverty. I was a single mother raising two sons when I adopted an infant girl, a maternal second cousin of mine, from foster care, and I could not catch a financial break.

In the mornings, I'd watch at least three of the televangelists' sermons back-to-back as the children and I got ready for work and school. One after another, they taught messages about seedtime and harvest. I did not know anything about agriculture, but I learned enough to know that reaping required sowing and if I wanted to reap a harvest of blessings, I needed to sow seeds of money. Now today that makes no sense to me, but then as a mom struggling to feed her kids, I would have believed anything to provide a better life for them. My pastor only talked about money at tithes and offering time, and then in such a way that the flow of money was unidirectional—me giving to God. And if I didn't give, Malachi 3 asserted that I was robbing God and that the devourer would eat what I withheld. The way I saw it, if I was financially struggling while giving my money, there was no way I could survive if I kept it for myself.

While the church taught sermons that encouraged its congregation to hold on, be strong, and wait for the Lord and the change that would come, televangelists taught that faith without works was dead. They taught that I needed to do something to get God to do something for me. Luke 6:38 was evidence of a bi-directional relationship between me and God, giving and receiving: "Give and it shall be given unto you..." I loved it that every last sermon of the televangelists was about money because I needed all of the reinforcement I could get. I held on to sermons about the parable of the talents—learning that if God gave me two talents I was responsible for at least doubling them. I loved the parable of the sower—learning that if I was going to sow my money, I needed to place it in "good" ground, not that which was thorny or stony. I stopped giving and loaning money to just anybody and only gave to those causes I knew that might yield a return, which was mostly the televangelists' churches. It all made sense then, although I can clearly hear the quackery in the theology now.

I lived for the praise reports, or testimonies from people who were not tithers or seed-sowers, and the blessings and miracles they received when they became so. There were pre-recorded videos of people talking about how God delivered them or their adult children from addiction or pornography. Others talked about how God granted them favor in court or some other predicament. My favorites were the ones who miraculously became debt-free. People talked about how unexpected checks or bags of money showed up and they were able to pay off their houses, cars, or student loans. One televangelist had us all repeating after him his catchphrase, "Money cometh!" I totally believed that if money came to those folks it would come to me, too, since God saw no differences between people.

The televangelists traveled all over the country, putting on or preaching at conferences. Whenever they came to Charlotte or within a two-hour distance, my best friends (they were financially strapped single mothers too) and I put our money together and gleefully went to their services. We loved being in the swollen auditoriums amidst the thick atmosphere of expectation. Experiencing the singing, teaching, and testimonies was otherworldly. Once I attended a televangelist's conference, desperate for a financial miracle. I enjoyed the breakout sessions on various topics such as church leadership, finding satisfaction in singleness, and strengthening prayer and devotion. Then, we all flocked to the convention stage to hear the sermon. I was awe-struck learning about the newly widowed single mother in 2 Kings 4 who went to the prophet asking for financial help. The prophet challenged her to use what she had in her house to get the money she needed. All she had was a little vial of oil, but the prophet gave instructions for a miraculous increase. The story ended with the woman paying all her debts, and her and her sons living off of the profits. I needed that kind of miracle, and I knew I had that widow's faith—that I had come to the conference with lack and debt but I would leave with an overflow of blessings.

The televangelist confirmed it when he told us that the same blessing was available for us. He asserted that we all had a little vial of oil that could miraculously be increased. He told us to get out our checkbooks or cash and prepare a gift indicative of the amount of oil we had. All I had was $100 in my checking account and I was willing to risk it all for an increase. As instructed, we held up our checks and cash in the air as the televangelist prayed over us. Then, the televangelist was interrupted by a message from the *Holy Spirit*. He thanked us for our gifts but told us that the holy spirit wanted us to pour it out. He mentioned that the widow's oil was not increased until she found the courage to pour it out. Paraphrasing, he said something like, "The holy spirit wants to bless your gift, but you need to pour it out, like a drink offering. Don't give to the Lord that which costs you nothing. The kind of financial breakthrough you need requires a zero on the end of the gift you were going to give." Putting an extra zero on the hundred dollars I intended to give meant that my check was going to bounce. I did not have $1000 in my checking account, but neither did the widow in the Bible and God blessed her and her children. I added a zero to my check and put it in the offering basket. I went home, where I spent three to four of my paychecks catching up from falling behind.

That might have made anybody else wise up, but not me. I attributed that mishap to not having enough faith. So, I worked on my faith. I kept giving to my church, the televangelists' ministries, and others who were in need. There were plenty of scriptures for me to recite as I gave, and one of my favorites reads, "He who scatters increases all the more, and he who withholds comes to poverty." I checked my mailbox neurotically looking for the fruit of the seeds I'd sown, or unexpected checks like the people in the pre-recorded videos. I even watched the ground where I walked looking for money, since there were lots of testimonies like those given at the conference or in the televangelists' monthly newsletters about people finding stacks of cash. I prayed for someone to show up behind me in the grocery store line and pay for my order, as in other reports from televangelist followers. My unexpected financial "breakthroughs" were not as grand as those, but they were enough to keep me going, and sowing.

For instance, one day I was fretting about how I was going to buy groceries for the week with only $20 cash. Out of the blue, one of my aunts telephoned me with regret for not coming to my housewarming party the year before and she wanted to know if she could stop by and drop off some groceries. Two hours later, my aunt unloaded an SUV full of groceries—meats, vegetables, breads, snacks, staples, and condiments. The kids and I had food for two weeks. I couldn't believe it; my sown seeds were sprouting! If that wasn't mind-blowing enough, another miracle happened when a colleague of mine called me to make good on a pledge we had made several years before. We vowed that if we ever decided to go into private practice, we would do it together. She called me up one day and said it was time. I told her I was financially strapped and would need a few more months before I could even think about taking such a risk. I wished her well in her new business and was ready to end the call. Instead, she invited me to the location where she wanted to set up her office. I went to celebrate with her and found that she had arranged for the property manager to meet us there. The space, a two-suite office with a spacious lobby and bathroom, would be perfect for us. While I shrank from disappointment in myself, my colleague told him we would meet him back there with our security deposit and first month's rent at 3pm on Friday. I was devastated and excited at the same time. I trusted that God would do something, because there was no way I would have $1100 in four days. I checked the mailbox every day, with excitement the first two days, out of desperation on the third day, and just out of habit on the final day. I am not lying when I write that a yellow DHL van pulled up to my house at 1pm on Friday with a $1300 certified check for me. It was a royalty check for the novel I had written a few years earlier. I was able to make good on the pledge and start my first business, building it from a two-woman show to a team of over 25 people with a six-figure revenue.

There were two things that broke me from the prosperity gospel. First, it began to sweep through Black churches, including the one I attended. Black pastors' sermons went from boosting us up to manage the weekly challenges we faced—as if we no longer needed healing in our bodies and godliness in our marriages and homes—to hosting high-dollar guest ministers whose messages about money led us to give. This was no problem, except that I saw people like me—financially struggling single parents, elderly people on fixed incomes, couples living paycheck to paycheck—giving their last so that God could bless them. I stopped seeing this kind of theology as something that would give something to me, seeing it instead as a means to take what I had and give it to somebody else. That too was scriptural according to the parable of the talents.

Black pastors began thriving, as evidenced by driving better cars and living in bigger homes and building new churches or enlarging the ones they had. Not long after, Black pastors started going to jail for tax evasion, tax fraud, and fraud. Black churches were being torn apart, devastated. Some members stayed at the church under new leadership, awaiting their pastor's release in eight or ten years, while others sought church homes elsewhere. Plots of land purchased for church expansion lay bare until overtaken by weeds and thorns while the pastors who purchased them fulfilled their sentences.

I eventually joined a church with a strong couples ministry. We loved learning from the trials and triumphs of David and Bathsheba, Samson and Delilah, Hosea and Gomer, Rebekah and Jacob, and Sarah and Abraham, to name a few. It was exactly what we needed for our blended family of eight—Nathan and I had three children apiece. After a couple of years, the church began to ask for money outside the tithes and offerings, which was understandable since the congregation was growing and we needed a bigger space to meet. Soon, the pastor began cracking jokes about money, one of which I understood and complied with. I laughed when he said, "Coming to the church without an offering is like showing up to someone's house empty handed every week, eating until you're full, and leaving. You should always bring something, even if it's $20." I wasn't offended by that statement, as the church had bills to pay, and the pastor's sermons were strengthening our family. Now, I can see how it opened the door for what was coming. Eventually, the church instituted twice-annual giving days where we would come with big gifts above our tithes and offerings.

I was okay with those projects too but the final straw for me was when we walked into the church for Big-Giving Sunday for what felt to me to be a spectacle. There was a lowered screen projector on the pulpit and two microphones had been set up on both sides of the altar. In lieu of a sermon, the pastor sat in the pulpit and asked us a question. "How do you think Jesus knew how much money the widow had when she put a mite in the offering plate?" The answer was, "Because he watched." So that Sunday he and his wife "watched" as we lined up on both sides of the church announcing the miracle we were believing God for and the amount of money we were giving when we got to the microphone. We were instructed, "Don't come up here with a million-dollar prayer request and a $20 bill." The gift needed to match our faith. We could see the numbers on the screen change as the announced amounts were calculated. Several hundreds of dollars were raised in less than two hours.

I felt perturbed and disgusted sitting in that audience, wondering how I'd gotten back to the prosperity gospel. I wanted to sit there in protest, but when it was time for our row to move forward it was more convenient to get up rather than have people slide over me. Plus, I worried what I looked like sitting there. My other source of anguish came from trying to figure out how much money I should give. I had money in my bank account this time, as my counseling practice was doing well, but I knew that I had money because I had stopped giving it away to the church. Nevertheless, I found it hard to stand at the microphone in front of the entire church and say I would not give any money. People who'd gone before me had given as little as $30 and others had given up to $13,000. I gave up my dignity along with a $1000 check.

I remain connected to the Bible and God. Interestingly enough, the older I got and the more life I experienced I conceptualized God as many different things: an ever-present energy, a woman, and Black. I was also changing, accepting myself as the same thing: alive and well as a Black woman. I figured how arrogant I must be to think that God is just white or just male. I think God is whatever someone needs God to be, when they need it. There are times when I need God to be something other than the wisdom and excellence of a Black woman. I might need a father figure or the strength or boldness of a man.

I could not imagine finding a church with such fluid perceptions of God, so I didn't even look when Nathan and I relocated to Florida. We attended the church of my husband's preference, and it took me a few Sundays and a lunch meeting with a person from the Black community to articulate my thoughts and reservations about the church. When my lunch mate asked if I had found a church home and I gave him the name of the church he said, "They don't know they're Black there." The immediate solidarity between us positively changed the dynamics of our first-time meeting. He even added depth to what I felt was a superficial dislike for the church. I thought I was bothered by the lifelessness of a 60-minute routine that included two songs, weekly announcements, a 20-minute sermon, an offering and altar call, and a song to end the service. I loved the fact that we went to the first service and had the rest of the day to ourselves. But the lunch mate talked about how the Black church had become corporatized into franchises. That made so much sense to me, as I could see evidence of it in the church we were attending. Having worked at McDonald's as a teen, I remember the angst our store felt when we were audited by headquarters, who sent representatives to ensure we showed fidelity to the restaurant's model. So, here we were in one of the satellite campuses that held fidelity to a predominantly white church that was headquartered in Alabama. It didn't matter that this offspring church had a Black pastor and mostly Black members, its service was whitewashed.

After I'd carefully navigated white spaces at work all week long, an exhausting exercise of discerning and dodging psychological landmines, I needed the restoration that comes from the Black church. Black gospel music reaches my soul and its singers know how to use their voices as instruments of healing, with runs, grovels, riffs, and expertly held notes. After years of despising the "hold on and be strong" messages I received in church earlier, I desperately needed those sermons now. With the series of events coming next for me, I needed the anchor of God with a Black-centered gospel while I reclaimed my Blackness.

Part 2
RECLAIMING MYSELF

CHAPTER 5

Black Again

I was jolted back to Blackness a few times before I fully embraced it. The first time I remember *feeling* Black was the night Trayvon Martin was murdered. The 17-year-old Black boy was walking through the gated, predominantly white community in Florida where he was allegedly visiting or staying with his father's fiancée. He was coming from a nearby convenience store with a bag of candy and a soft drink when he realized he was being followed. George Zimmerman, a 28-year-old resident of the community and the organizer of its neighborhood watch program, followed Trayvon while on the phone with the police. An alleged scuffle broke out between the two and ended when Zimmerman fatally shot Martin.

Up until this point in my racial identity development, being heavily entrenched in internalized racism, whenever I heard news of an atrocity against the Black community I would simply feel sadness or sympathy, and gratitude for being removed from environments where I or my children might meet the same fate. But Trayvon wasn't shot in the "hood," and I realized that the white suburban community where we lived provided no more protection for my children than the one that housed Trayvon's family. Even scarier to me was that my firstborn son was 16, close to Trayvon's age, and my middle child was a towering 14-year-old boy in a man's 6'5 frame and he lived in hoodies like the one Trayvon had been wearing. For the first time, I thought to myself *that could have been one of my sons.*

I wanted to be the first to talk to my children about the shooting, so I did not waste time giving them *the talk*. I felt foolish for saying things like, "You are Black," "Things are different for you," and, "The girls love your 6'5 frame but to some people, particularly white people, your height is a threat." These words felt like gravel coming up from the pit of my stomach. They felt like contradictions as they were quite different from what I had taught them as they were growing up and we moved into white spaces. I'd said things like, "You're no different from anybody else. You can do anything they can do. You are just as good as, and even better than the kids in your class and this community. You always remember that." But Trayvon's murder showed me that my words meant nothing outside my house, and that I should have had *the talk* with my children earlier. Most Black parents begin introducing their children to age-appropriate concepts about race, identity, and how to interact with the police at elementary school age. Research shows that children begin to develop racial attitudes as early as six and seven years old, which corresponds with the age that Black children first realize they are Black. Here I was, near 40, reckoning with my own racial identity.

It may have been a knee-jerk response, but I took my children out of the predominantly white private schools where they had been studying and enrolled them in nearby schools where there were more Black children, for reinforcement and support. That is the thing with racial identity development, encountering race-based incidents elicits a response that either moves us further along the development continuum or we make choices that cause us to regress or stay stuck where we are. It is not a linear process, and sometimes there is progression or regression. I encourage any reader who is not familiar with racial identity development to explore Dr. William Cross' work on The Nigresence Model, and Dr. Janet Helms' work on White Racial Identity Development. I wonder how different I would be if I had been introduced to it early on and taught that my status as a Black woman wasn't a double whammy but an asset. When I was younger I strove to find out how white people lived but at this point in my ethinc identity development I became aware that there was a Black world out there that my children did not know.

You should have seen me checking my children for bruises and other evidence of fighting or mischief when they returned home from the predominantly Black schools those first few days. I was worried as heck about them. I had worked hard to not lose them to the streets, and I wanted them to be different from my father, cousins, and uncles. My sons would be the first boys from my biological family to graduate high school, and I recognized that with our bloodline that would be no easy feat. I felt a responsibility to protect and foster them, to turn the tide of generational curses into a lineage of goodness and success. Today, having progressed along the latter ends of racial identity development, I can easily detect the self-righteousness, self-hatred, and ignorance in my beliefs. I am ashamed to reflect on those experiences and admit that I sent my children to white schools and asked them nothing other than, "How was your day?" or, "What did you learn?" Knowing what I know now, I would have asked more pointed questions such as, "What's your relationship with your teachers like? Do you feel heard and seen at your school? How do your peers refer to you? Are your needs met at that school, and are you happy there?" Race-based experiences don't carry the kind of scars or bruises I was looking for. I would have needed to assess them differently.

Having the children in predominantly Black schools led us to growth in other ways. It forced us to look at other intersections of our lives besides race. For instance, I had not considered talking to the children about my political affiliation. One day, I was minding my business and preparing dinner when the firstborn came home and told me I owed him money. When I inquired more, this child had the nerve to tell me that the parents of his friends at the new school paid their children. "My friends' mommas claim them on their taxes and give them money for it." My son had never been fresh in the mouth or talked back to me, but I found this claim to be funny. Boldly he said, "I'm wondering why I'm just now hearing about tax money. You owe me a lot of money." Flippantly, I laughed and said, "Child, tell your friends we're Republicans." I didn't realize how loaded that admission was, and it warranted another talk.

Within it I had to recall how I had drifted away from a family of Democrats. My entire family were Democrats, both biological and adopted. At 18 years old, I cast my first vote for a straight Democratic ticket as I did every year after. However, after leaving the women's shelter and living on my own for a little while, I moved in with my parents so I could get help with the kids and save up money. My commute to work was a 75-minute drive and I stayed awake to and from work by listening to a Christian talk radio station. I didn't know that it was conservative or what that even meant, but I fell in love with shows like "Focus on the Family" and "Money Matters." I listened to advice for raising adult children, dealing with spouses who were addicted to pornography or who were unbelievers, and how to set boundaries in co-dependent relationships. "Money Matters" was my favorite show and I loved hearing people call in about money problems such as school loan debt, high car payments, underemployment, and so on. The radio host incorporated scriptures into his advice and advised people to pay back their debt as it was ungodly to not pay back what was entrusted to you. I knew the values were totally different from my own, but I was attracted to messages of self-reliance, industriousness, living debt-free, trustworthiness, not looking for handouts, and not being the borrower but the lender. I even heard radio shows endorsing Republican presidential candidates because of their Christian and pro-life beliefs. I changed my political party affiliation and began voting Republican, until I voted for President Barack Obama for both of his terms. Now, I know that the values I adopted then were Eurocentric and did not consider the systemic barriers I faced. I was oppressing myself trying to live by those standards.

My children excelled socially at the predominantly Black schools. Their friends at school also lived in our neighborhood, so they were able to hang out at home rather than having to drive across town for social gatherings. The children loved being with their people and their vocabulary changed as they learned slang, popular sayings, and walked like they had swag. It was right up my middle child's alley, as he had conformed to the private school attire and code of conduct with disdain. Taking note of their Blackness one of my friends gifted the boys with a Lil' Wayne CD. You could not tell them that they were not bonafide rappers as they rapped along to the artist's clever rhymes, masterful analogies, and irresistible beats. I was happy for them.

I made a lot of mistakes while stepping back into Blackness, one of which was comparing the diverse schools to the white one we had come from. The children rarely had homework. I was used to them coming home from the private school with hours of assignments to complete for most of their subjects. But now they rarely brought books home. Actually, my first-born did not have books. His school was sorely underfunded, and their books were on jump drives. I did my best to overlook these things and offset my concerns by participating in the parent–teacher associations (PTAs) at each school. That was another difference from the private school. The PTA meetings were full of parents at the private school but attendance was lower at the community schools. With an ethnocentric lens, I understand that parents at the community schools had to work, may have had transportation barriers, and may have had fewer resources than our private school counterparts. Never-theless, I noticed that parents came out to the football games and I caught them there when I got fired up about some news I wanted to use to make a difference. The graduation rate at the community school was 55 percent. That was appalling to me and frightening, because the following year I would have two sons at the school and with a half-chance for success, it meant that one of my sons would not graduate from the school. That would have been the realization of one of my worst fears.

A predominantly white school about 20 minutes away touted a 97 percent graduation rate. There, they had books, real bleachers and not the aluminum seats at my alma mater where I registered my firstborn to attend; the campus was well manicured, while the grass and shrubbery at my son's school was as dead as the school's budget. The restaurants around the white schools supported it and they kept *Go Bulldogs!* on their billboards. When the white school teams won their away games, the parents lined the street to the school and shouted, clapped, and held up poster signs as the bus crept down the street past them into the school. There was nothing like that around my alma mater. I used the last quarters of my son's schooling at my alma mater to make a difference. I called the few restaurants near the school—Arby's, Hardee's, and Subway—and asked if they would encourage the students with a *Go Hawks!* greeting. Only one agreed, but I was grateful for that one. I began talking to parents at the football games to see if they were interested in creating a welcome wall when the boys got back from games, whether they won or lost (because most of their games ended in a loss, which was even more of a reason to encourage them). The parents thought that was *white shit*. And, when I talked with them about the graduation rate they told me to take my ass to the 97 percent school then. I later recognized my mistake; I did what white advocates do. They look in from a deficits lens and tell folks what they need to make their place better, and even worse they do so when they have not established a relationship with the people who live there. Ouch! These are just a few of the bumps and bruises I got while progressing along the path to racial identity development.

In order for my children to attend the white public school

with higher graduation rates, I needed to live in a community within the district. It was not easy to find affordable housing there. But I was determined to make sure my children had access to resources their white counterparts had. I rented a townhouse that was almost double the cost of my mortgage. I joked to my husband, "This is how they keep the Black people out." The fact that I thought it was a joke was indicative of where I was racial identity-wise. Because today I understand that it's called redlining. Redlining is a form of discrimination where mortgage and insurance loans and other financial services are denied to people of color, with intent to keep them in certain communities and schools. I was learning again how costly passing for white could be. Being racially colorblind made me oblivious to the racial microaggressions, invalidations, and insults I endured. Ignorantly, I chalked racism up to white people's ignorance and viewed it as an indication that I needed to work harder to prove that I belonged in their spaces. If it cost more, I paid it. If it hurt more, I took it. I would not offer my children what cost me nothing. Little did I know that overlooking racism would cost them too.

Like the time I thought I was doing my firstborn a favor by having him get to know the white male principal at the predominantly white private middle school, I found out what the principal's favorite things were through his secretary. Every Monday, I sent my son to the principal's office with a different item from the list: a six-pack of Dr. Pepper soft drinks, or a bag of trail mix, or a bag of chili cheese Fritos, or an inspirational book on leadership. My intentions were pure: I wanted that principal to know my son, and I wanted my son to know what it felt like going to the principal's office without trouble being a reason. I was a single mother at the time and raising a teenage Black son at a conservative, Christian school, I had no idea what to expect, but if my son did get into trouble I needed this principal to know his character. Looking back, I wonder if I set my son up for the events that would unfold. Maybe my actions made this white principal think I probably had an angle, that my son was probably a troublemaker and that I was buttering him up, or that I was trying to earn brownie points. The fact that my son was a straight-A student, a stellar athlete, and a respectful young man should have been enough for me to know that my son might have never been sent to the principal's office or that if he did, we could handle it together. But, my childhood had only prepared me to prevent trouble rather than to resolve it. So I groomed my children to not get in trouble because I knew I did not have the power or resources to get them out of it. This is a second parental regret I have, directly behind teaching the children to be racially colorblind.

So, a year later, in the spring of my son's seventh grade year, the principal called for me to come and pick my son up for a three-day suspension. When I got to the school, my son was sitting there with his head held down and a note the principal told him to give me. "Read it," the principal demanded. I read the first couple of lines, "My name is Floweezy and I'm here to stay, I fucked my science teacher the other day..." I looked at my son, "What is this?" He looked up at me and with a quiet voice told me it was a rap. He and one of his classmates were starting a rap group. I closed the letter and gathered my son. The principal stopped me and insisted, "Read the entire rap." I looked at the angry smirk on the principal's face and couldn't understand where it came from. If anybody was supposed to be angry, it was me. My son had been called to his office for trouble, the very thing I was trying to prevent. Still in the phase of my life where I was passing for white, I complied and read the rap—the other 20 or so lines were no different from the first line. Sure, I was upset because the lyrics were explicit but to me, as a practicing mental health therapist and a mom, it was age appropriate. "I'm appalled that he would speak about his teacher in that way," the principal said. I agreed that it was offensive but it was a rap from a 13-year-old boy about sex, and what middle schooler wasn't crushing on their teachers? Seeing that the principal was visibly upset led me to believe that I wasn't taking it as seriously as I should so the understanding I had toward my son turned into anger against him. I gave him a good tongue lashing for embarrassing me in front of that white man, and I put him on punishment after admonishing him to use his words for good. It wasn't until years later when I was a whole Black woman rethinking incidents of my life that I realized the principal's excessive anger could have been because my son talked about sleeping with a white women. White people's age-old fear that Black men rape white woman is ludicrous but still alive. I regretted that I did not better advocate for my son and I wish I had renegotiated that three-day suspension, and brought to the principal's awareness what I perceived as racism. Now I am able to see that my son was exploring a creative side of himself that had come to him from both of his grandparents—Brother Ali and Brenda had dabbled in poetry, with Ali being the most prolific. I hate that my inability to confront the principal led me to lash out at my son, and I distinctly remember saying, "Leave white women the hell alone." Then, I got mad at myself because how could I expect my son to leave white women alone when I was trying to be one?

The encounter of racism that led me to fully embrace Blackness occurred when I was a student in a doctoral program, studying counselor education and supervision after 20-plus years of mental health and addictions experience in the community. I was just proud to have been accepted as one of eight students for such a program. I was the second oldest, one of two Black students, and the one with the most experience and a thriving clinical counseling business in the community. I loved learning how to think, write, teach, and present like a scholar, and even though it was a learning curve, I happily accepted the challenge.

I remember during one of our many crying episodes, my cohort members and I were sharing our experiences. I cried telling them how much being a doctorate student meant to me. "When I grab my purse, it means I'm taking care of my family. When I grab my laptop bag, it means I'm taking care of my staff and our clients. But, when I grab this bookbag, it means I'm doing something for me. It's the only thing I have that's mine." That self-fulfilment kept me going through the program. So when my first paper from a seminar class was returned to me with zero points and a note that read, "Rewrite. This is not scholarly writing at all," I turned my frustration into a brilliantly written three-page research paper about why that doctoral seminar course was a waste of money based on literature from scholarly journals. I earned 100 points and probably became the target that professor continued to aim for and hit throughout my academic journey.

That one professor was brilliant, a specialist in our field, and I respected her. But I could not understand why she always felt the need to state her role in the department when she spoke with me. I knew her role and I knew she knew I knew, but for whatever reason she needed to tell me, every time. I came to understand that she was putting me in my place. It's a thing that Black people experience when white people feel threatened and I have experienced it in the forms of a threat, being overlooked for a promotion, and having support withheld. Something to let me know that I had gotten too big for my britches, and needed to be reminded of my lowly state. During the Jim Crow era if a Black person was too proud, too clean, had too much, or drove or lived better than a white person believed they should, white people believed that person needed to be taken down a peg or two or be put in their place. As a result, their house or business would be set on fire or there would be some other consequence aimed at lowering them.

One attempt to lower me came when this professor called me into her office. I was excited, thinking she was going to do for me what I'd heard she'd done for others—take me under her wing or ask me to collaborate with her on a project. After small talk, she told me that she liked Black people. I wasn't sure how to respond so I let her talk. She listed the names of Black students, including the one in my cohort and others in cohorts above mine—everyone except me. Since she was on a roll, I suggested the name of a Black woman student I knew who graduated two years prior. With disgust in her voice she said, "No, not her." I didn't ask any questions, but I thought about that student—statuesque with her dark-skinned face accentuated by lavender-glossed lips and a tiny platinum blond afro.

Every head turned when this Black woman entered rooms and she took up space. She was not known to cower or mince her words. I could see how she would end up on this professor's do-not-like list—but me? Aside from my skin complexion, I am the complete opposite of that student. I am what my biological mother called "meek mouthed," meaning I didn't speak up for myself. I am mousy—hence not responding to this woman's confession of liking certain Black people. I shrink back, avoid conflict, and adhere to respectability politics when it comes to hair and clothing. There was nothing about me that would warrant being on this professor's hit list. I ended the conversation after the professor told me that she had Black friends and that they come to her house. "Yes, they look after my mother when she is sick." I stood up and made a beeline for the door, wishing I had the confidence to tell her that those were not friends, they were *the help*.

I'm not sure if the next attempt to lower me was planned or not, but in class my cohort members and I were preparing our dissertation topics. One by one we were called to stand at the podium and type out our prospectus titles on the computer so the class and professor could see them on screen. The professor gave helpful suggestions as students talked through their plans. When it was my turn, I nervously stood up at the podium because I wasn't quite sure that I had arrived at the topic I wanted to study. Each word appeared on the screen as I typed *The Impact of Power, Race, and Gender on the Cross-Racial Supervisory Relationship*. While I was talking through my study, the professor stood up, walked to the podium where I was, moved me out of the way with her being and said, "I have something better for you to study." She typed over the words in my title, she removed the word *race*, and explained why her revised title and study was better suited for me. I conceded and sat down, as she began to explain my new topic to the class. She asked me to come finish my work. I sat there with my hands on my head, trying to figure out what was happening, and how I should respond. I could not process what I was feeling or experiencing but a white woman cohort member verbalized it after class when she said, "LaTonya, I'm sorry you were bullied."

That was a great word to describe that incident and the ones to follow. By the time that woman had finished with me, I graduated with a degree and an antidepressant. I had been lowered. But my road back to Blackness came in the form of an advanced multicultural counseling course taught by a woman faculty of color (as most of these classes are, which is a perfect example of tokenism). I do not even remember the subject matter that day, but I do recall internally processing what she and my cohort members were talking about, and surprising myself when I spoke my thoughts aloud. "So, you mean to tell me that I can bring my Blackness into this room as well as my intellect?" I realized that I wasn't just pondering the question to myself when all heads turned toward me. I had never had an outburst or spoken out of turn, and I sat there bewildered. Pained. Vulnerable. But feeling Black again.

The question I'd accidentally asked in class ended in a lilt of heavy sadness as I recognized the weight of the words and the harm I'd inflicted on myself all those years assimilating, stretching, and pressing for whiteness, all while leaving, denying, and suppressing my Black self. I had never acknowledged, let alone confessed, that I intentionally left my Blackness in my childhood. I sat there and cried; I mourned my losses. I wept for trading the richness of Grandma Louise's values for the poverty of self me and my white mentors celebrated. I wailed for believing that my children and I were safer in spaces where there were white people than the places where there were people who looked like us, and for thinking I'd won when I made it to spaces where I was the only Black person in the room. I mourned for getting my dialect so down pat that if somebody closed their eyes they wouldn't know it was a Black woman speaking.

I wished I'd had the sense of David when in the Bible he said no when Saul loaned him battle attire to fight against the giant Goliath. David tried on the gear but the weight of it was too much for him to bear. "I cannot go in these," he announced. Instead, he used what he had on his person—a slingshot and five smooth stones. He slayed the giant of his life with a toy-turned-weapon. If I had known that white values were not a good fit for me, and that all I needed was the courage of the four-year-old girl inside me who fought to survive and lived, I too would have slayed giants much earlier than now.

CHAPTER 6

Black Lives Matter

*I*t was as if 2020 rode in on a horse with a vendetta against Black people, and I didn't see its white-hooded face coming. I was too busy anticipating a year of perfection, symmetry, and perfect vision. I expected that living in a double-digit year would mean living in alignment and balance, just as perfectly as the number 2020 reflected itself. *This is going to be my best year yet*, I remember thinking to myself and tweeting it to others.

I was already sick before COVID-19 infected the world. Proof of my insanity could be found in a day's page of my at-a-glance calendar where I prayed daily for energy to triage an ungodly number of meetings and tasks. My stomach was always in knots that I tried to untie with Mylanta, Tums, herbal teas, and flaxseed oil. With as much money as I spent at the counter for ibuprofen trying to get rid of near daily headaches, I could have bought stock in a pain reliever company and had money to spare. I lost hair and gained weight, trying to find my place as a first-generation Black woman in academia. I felt like a fish out of water, and I guess my body got tired of putting up with a mouth that said yes to everything because of a mind that couldn't discern the difference between a dead-end assignment and one that would lead to something greater.

Passing for white was more exhausting than embracing myself as a Black woman, because then just as I did when I was a child, I took the blame for and the responsibility to fix whatever was wrong. But, as a full-bodied Black woman in the Ivory Tower with my eyes and ears wide open, I carried the weight of navigating a white world on my shoulders, neck, and back and could feel the pressure in my chest. I found academia to be a minefield, just as I'd read and heard, related to the challenges Black faculty faced in their pursuit of tenure and promotion. To combat this, one of the first things I did when I stepped foot on the predominantly white institution (PWI) where I was newly employed was to seek out other Black faculty. I was dismayed to find that I made the third Black professor out of nearly 300 faculty. I then assumed that the Black student body was low. However, at a beginning-of-the-year ceremony for first-year students, I saw so many Black students walking into the event it felt as if I was in a twilight zone. Clearly, I did not ask enough questions about diversity and inclusion during my interviewing and onboarding process.

My experiences at the university had been good, even from the beginning. I was asked to sit on committees in my department and across campus, be photographed or visible at university events in the community, and provide diversity training across the campus to faculty and student groups. I added to my plate the things I wanted to do, like Sister to Sister, the affinity group I created for women students of color. I wanted students of color to know that there were faculty of color on that campus, in addition to the people of color they saw serving food in the cafeteria and cleaning up the buildings. We three Black faculty members taught at the graduate level and it did not sit well with me that the undergraduate Black student population (a whopping 43%) could spend four years at the university and not touch a Black faculty member, and that the white student body would not be able to sit under a Black professor but would be expected to enter a workforce where there would be Black colleagues.

I found that working passionately to champion diversity left me exhausted by my third year of employment in academia, right when my pre-tenure dossier was required. This compilation would show whether I was on track for tenure and promotion or not. So, I asked for dossiers from peers who had successfully passed that part of the process so I could use their portfolios as a guide. I studied their portfolios, especially those who worked within my department, and I found the ones outside my department just as helpful. My colleagues had compressed three years of work into 78–178-page portfolios, with the lowest number of pages belonging to the one white male faculty member who agreed to let me use his dossier. I figured mine, the first dossier of a Black person that my dean and department review committee would have ever seen, needed to be extraordinary and fall at the longer end. I ended up with a 283-page document showcasing my teaching, research, and service to my department, the university, the community, and across the country. The swelling in my chest was not pride as I presumed it would be, but anger. While my colleagues congratulated me for submitting such *amazing* work, I couldn't match their energy. "That's impressive," one of them said. "Congratulations, you've worked your tail off," said another. One of them stopped long enough to notice my pursed lips and raised eyebrow. "What's wrong, you're not proud of yourself?" I was surprised by my answer but I didn't have the energy to filter it or care, "I feel like I'm tap dancing for white people." After I uploaded my dossier and hit submit on the online platform, I went home and crashed. I literally couldn't get out of bed, my body acted as though it had run a marathon and collapsed at the finish line. I was tearful from fatigue and there was a pressure behind my nose, eyes, and cheekbones as if someone had punched my entire face. My nose was congested and runny, and my throat was sore.

I rarely got sick, so I had not been in a hurry to establish a medical home with a local primary care physician after my relocation. I took my complaints to the nearest urgent care center. When I was called back, I did all the preliminary stuff— weight check and blood pressure. Then, I was instructed to lean back so the nurse could stick a long cotton swab into my nostril until it tickled the back of it. That caused me to sneeze in his face which I thought was the nastiest thing. I apologized and said, "If that thing makes people sneeze in your face, you should be wearing a mask." The physician came in after him and she told me that my strep and flu tests had come back negative. She diagnosed me with a sinus infection and gave me prescriptions for a saline nasal spray, an antibiotic, and a medication for cough. "I don't have a cough," I told her. "You might develop one. And, when you do, take that." I filled the prescriptions, went home and got into bed, where I gave myself permission to stay until I had the courage to work differently. I was not going to let academia kill me. Spring break would be next week, and I planned to use it to strategize my next moves, but then COVID-19 hit.

I did not know what to make of the pandemic. I had never even heard of the word, and emotionally I was caught between embracing a two-week break and panicking about the world coming to an end. With edicts from the powers-that-be for people to stay at home, stay off the roads, and to be in the house by a certain time unless you had documentation verifying your status as an essential worker, I couldn't catch my bearings. I was not a news-watcher, but it was hard not to watch to stay in the know about precautions and hope for this whole thing ending. With the numbers of people infected with coronavirus on one end of the television screen and the number of deaths on the other end, I felt as if I was in the movie *The Hunger Games*. It felt as if someone was behind a computer orchestrating a survival of the fittest contest. There was even a prediction that by the time this thing was over everyone would know someone who had been infected with the coronavirus.

Two weeks into the pandemic and the issue of US race relations had reared its ugly head. First, it was the way in which the news about COVID was disseminated to Black communities. Tweets and posts such as, "Black people don't worry, you can't catch COVID. You have melanin," permeated our Twitter and social media feeds. There was a short-lived collective exhale. We were grateful that Black Jesus had dispensed superpowers associated with our genetic makeup. We watched the news as it released breaking stories about newly diagnosed celebrities. Tom Hanks and his wife Rita were diagnosed with COVID. By the time Black people found out that melanin was not an antidote to the coronavirus, it was too late. Our communities were ravaged by the virus. The death toll for Black people surpassed the number of white deaths. The immunity hypothesis, a component of medical racism from the 1800s, had struck again. Back then, it was said that Black people did not need mental health care since they did not own property or businesses and they did not engage in civil affairs such as voting, so they were immune from mental illness. The immunity hypothesis still hurts Black communities today, as the number of deaths by suicide among Black youth has exceeded the total number of deaths by suicide among white youth.

Soon hospitals across the country were overcrowded with victims who were in the throes of COVID, and people who were afraid their bodies might be the next incubators for the virus. I read the newspaper headlines but did not have the mental bandwidth to read the stories. The headlines were enough to know how to direct my prayers and my work. One headline read that hospitals were so overwhelmed doctors would be permitted to choose whom to administer care to. That headline punched me in my stomach, as I grasped at my chest to catch my breath. The immunity hypothesis among physicians manifests in a belief that Black people are strong and they do not experience pain in the same way that white people do. It is also believed that Black people are drug seekers, so even when they do seek help for pain they are less likely to receive medications, or are given lower dosages of medications. If doctors were to choose the people to administer care to, I knew the death toll among Black people would increase. News permeated our communities reporting that Black people were sent home from hospitals without treatment, or were dying while waiting for care, or were cared for with less rigorous treatment plans and regimens.

Access to healthcare wasn't the only disparity illuminated by COVID. Issues such as insurability, who could be deemed as essential workers, exposure to COVID, and what activities were deemed essential came to light. I would have never paid attention to any of this when I was passing for white. I would have patted myself on the back for making it out of the hood and no longer living paycheck to paycheck. And I would have uttered a prayer for Black people that God would protect them and bless them with opportunities for advancement like those given to me. But this fully Black me knew I hadn't made it alone, or solely with God's help. I was standing on a lot of Black shoulders and I felt a responsibility to pay it back (or forward, and sometimes both). I had an obligation to do something good with the privileges I had been given.

While my family of origin were essential workers, I was in Florida where it seemed that some residents did not know or care that a pandemic was in effect. Florida beaches were full of people surfing, sunbathing, and enjoying their families and friends while we were supposed to be social distancing. When the county closed our beaches, residents got on the news and advocated for themselves. "We need this beach open for our mental health," I heard one woman say. I thought about the disparities along the continuum of oppression and privilege. While one set of folks had to work and keep themselves and their families safe from COVID, another set of folks were petitioning to re-open the beach. It was astounding to me.

Due to social distancing, the kids in the community where

I lived could not play basketball. A couple of times I saw them defy the rules and play anyway. Not too long after, my husband Nathan and I drove past the basketball court on our way to an appointment and the police were taking down the basketball nets. We reached our destination, an attorney's office, to complete paperwork on the purchase of our home. Once there, wearing disposable masks and gloves, we tried to make ourselves comfortable. I looked out of the attorney's office window and noticed that it sat on a beautiful golf course. Then, I noticed a handful of players. "I thought we were supposed to be social distancing." The lilt on the end of my statement made it sound like more of a question and it hid the disgust in my tone. "Oh, golf is essential." The way I sat up in my chair made Nathan tap me on the knee. "Not now, Sojourner Truth," he whispered. So, I waited until our paperwork was signed, and then I kindly made sure the attorney knew that if the Black kids in our community could not play basketball then the white men outside his window should not be out there playing golf.

As it turns out, 2020 did happen to be the year of perfect vision as we saw perfectly that we were not living in a post-racist society. We may have hoped that the 2008 election of President Barack Obama meant an end to racism and hatred. But, for many Black people, their experiences living in America worsened. COVID, on the other hand, was a gasoline set to a covert spark. We were slightly into the pandemic when news of Ahmaud Arbery's untimely and unjust death by ambush broke. I wasn't able to catch my breath between fears—when I wasn't fearing that my parents might catch COVID, I was worried that my sons might get stopped by the police or some other white person. My breath was snatched away again by the news of

Breonna Taylor's death, as if it came to me to say, *Don't think your daughter is exempt from being killed*. Now while there was a resemblance between my firstborn and Ahmaud, my chubby, baby-hair-lined-faced daughter and Breonna could have been twins—same height, weight, complexion, with a nose ring in the same place, and both were attached to boyfriends who might be of interest to law enforcement officers. I was beside myself with worry. I was restless, going on aimless drives to soothe myself, constantly cleaning the house and organizing closets and cabinets, and praying like a madwoman that God would protect my family. To add salt to an already open wound, news of George Floyd's death rang out. I did not watch the videos showcasing Ahmaud's, Breonna's, or George's deaths. Because of my childhood wounds, I am unable to watch videos of fights, people cursing and arguing, or anything else resembling things I endured as a child. My entire nervous system responds from being triggered and my ability to rebound requires much psychological work. If hearing that George Floyd called out for his mother was triggering for me, I cannot imagine what actually hearing him call for her might do to me. Just the thought of a 46-year-old man calling out for his mother in a time of trouble breaks my heart, and learning that she was already deceased broke me.

It was painful to be Black, but not in the bemoaning way I experienced it as a child, wanting to run from it. In the fullness of Blackness, that pain felt like a privilege and a rite of passage so I simply permitted myself to feel it and to sit in it, believing and knowing that it was beautiful to be Black.

I had shown up to the university with a hair weave because there was no way my fine spongy hair could withstand

Florida's humidity. On the second day of my interview, a faculty member looked at my natural wispy, once-curled hair and said, "See, you already have Florida hair." I fixed that with a sewn-in chin-length bob. Sometimes I spiced up the straight hairstyle by having ocean wave hair installed instead. Weaves were convenient and I loved not having to do my hair, because I was not good at it anyway. Brenda had been a cosmetologist when she was younger, but I did not inherit any of her skills. I cannot part hair straight, braid, or use curling or flat irons. When I was raising my daughter Destiny, I was always afraid that someone would call the child welfare system on me because it was not unusual for her hair to be unkempt.

At the university, the longer I was there, the more Black students were attracted to our program. Soon, I had classes with two or three Black women, and two or three Black men. I loved it, and I loved receiving notes and emails from them about how it made them feel to have a Black professor. The young Black women in the program were unapologetically Black. They didn't feel the need to overdress, straighten their hair, or subscribe to any of the respectability politics I had abided by. I started feeling bad about wearing weaves since my Black women students showed up to class proudly wearing their natural hair in beautiful locs, twists, and updos. I wanted to show them that they could advance in this predominantly white profession with their natural hair. I didn't get the courage to do anything differently to my hair until the pandemic, and then it was only because I developed a medical condition.

"No, it *is* psoriasis," my Asian American woman dermatologist repeated, with emphasis on the *is*. "But, it can't be," I pleaded. "There's no cure for that." I wasn't in denial because the silvery scales on my scalp, hairline, eyebrows, and ears were mild enough that they could barely be seen on my dark skin. My core thought was, *Damn, something else I got to live with*. The dermatologist recommended a three-day wash regimen which was ungodly for a Black woman, especially one with a weave. I was already sullen by the time Nathan and I reached the parking lot. He permitted me to fret about how much of a waste of money it would be to keep any hairstyle with a three-day wash regimen. "I ought to just cut it off," I said. Nathan vehemently protested. He tried making me feel better, and by that time we were in the pharmacy looking for Vitamin D. He joked, "I know the doctor prescribed 4000 milligrams of Vitamin D. But you don't need those pills. I got a Vitamin D that will clear all of that up." We both laughed at his wicked sense of humor. Of course he thinks he is the remedy for all that ails me, but I take those vitamins religiously.

We got home and I headed straight for the bathroom. I cried, staring at myself in the six-bulb Hollywood-style vanity mirror. I retrieved a pair of scissors from a drawer underneath the sink and held them up to my head. I found the thread from a sewn-in track of hair to cut. Nathan walked in and gingerly took the scissors out of my hand, pulled me into his chest, and let me cry. A couple of hours later, he announced that he would go and pick up dinner for us since neither of us was in the mood to cook. As soon as I heard the garage door close, I went straight to those scissors and cut the weave out of my hair. I could have stopped there, but once I had my natural hair out, I decided to cut it off, too. I cut it down just above my scalp. The shortest length my hair had ever been, and I heard a concoction of voices—the childhood taunts from my mother that included words like bald-headed, nappy headed, and popeyed. I stood in the mirror, teary-eyed, with a reflection of Brenda looking back at me. I looked everything like her—big doe eyes, full lips, prominent high cheekbones, and a set of naturally pointed eyebrows that made us look angry. *I'm just like her*, I thought to myself, remembering the time she pulled out a pair of clippers and shaved her head bald because she couldn't get her hair to look right that day. I was probably ten years old the first time I saw her do it. I stood at her side, horrified as she laughed and cried, all at the same time. "How do I look?" she asked with a smile as she turned her patchy bald head from side to side. I knew better than to insult her, so I didn't answer.

I did not feel beautiful with short hair, but I had meetings, presentations, and lessons I needed to show up for and teach or facilitate. Nobody said anything about my new look, and I imagined they probably thought the same thing I thought about my mother—*this girl done lost it*. I stopped concerning myself with what they thought and turned my worry toward whether or not I would be able to move up at the university with a teeny-weeny afro. I did not get a doctorate degree to be a professor for the rest of my life. I wanted to be a university president, particularly at a historically Black college or university (HBCU). It didn't make much sense to me that predominantly white institutions had a plethora of resources while some HBCUs struggled to keep the lights on. I planned to learn as much as I could and take it to improve HBCUs. I went to the internet and pulled pictures of Black women university presidents. Not that there were a lot of them, but among the ones I did find, a whopping 90 percent had relaxed or straightened hair. I only found two of them with natural hair—one with locs and the other with a short afro, which was a little longer than mine. I got the message loud and clear—if I wanted to be a university president, I would not be able to do it with natural hair. Instead of just worrying about it, I decided to test my theory.

I spoke to a colleague of mine at Northwestern University, who had recently cut off her relaxed tresses and was growing out her hair into a natural afro. She called me upset one day after a white colleague had referred to her as *Dr. Sassy*. "How come my hair always has to be the topic of discussion? Can't I just show up with a different hairstyle and not be called a name? So, I'm no longer Dr. Davis because my hair is natural?" That was not too long before I cut my hair off and decided to study the phenomenon. She happily agreed to be my co-investigator. I was so excited that I mentioned the study in class and one of my students, a Bosnian American male, asked if he could help. So, the three of us designed a quantitative study for early-career Black women who wore their natural hair to work while looking for advancement in their careers. We applied for a grant and received funding to carry out our research. Using focus groups, we interviewed 12 Black women from various professions across the country and after analyzing data we learned three things: Black women had to negotiate their identities at work in ways their white counterparts did not. For example, while many prospective candidates might focus on what they are going to say during their job interviews, the Black women in the study focused on what hairstyle and clothing they should wear, knowing that if they were too Black, they might not get the job. Once employed, many of them let their hair down so to speak, but not too much, as *tone it down* was another theme that emerged. Black women monitored their

facial expressions, volume of voice and hair, and their clothing, understanding that their appearance deemed them professional or not. Another theme that emerged was *double standards*,
wherein the grooming standards at work were different for
Black women than their white counterparts. "A white woman
can show up at work with red or purple hair but when I do
it, I am called into the office for being distracting," one par-
ticipant had said. Another commented, "I can wear the same
dress that a white woman wears but mine will be looked on
as unprofessional and unsuitable for the office because I have
bigger hips than she does." In terms of natural hair bias, every
last one of the women talked about how their co-workers and
clients touched their hair without permission, made their hair
the topic of discussion, and that they knew Black women who
had left the place of employment because their natural hair
kept them from promotion. None of the women worked at
places where Black women were in leadership. I felt proud to
disseminate the results of our study in a peer-reviewed journal and at national conferences wearing my own natural hair,
validating the experiences of Black women in our audiences. It
no longer mattered to me whether or not I would advance at
the university or become a university president. I'd found that
I could positively impact Black people without a higher title.

Becoming a whole Black woman for me feels like Celie's
journey to self in Steven Spielberg's *The Color Purple*. So many of
Celie's lines deeply resonated with me throughout my life. At
times when I'd let people take advantage of me or had given too
much of myself to someone or something, in my head I'd hear
Celie's sister Nettie tell her, "Don't let them run over you. You
got to fight." To which Celie replies, "I don't know to fight. All

I know how to do is stay alive." Staying alive is my superpower. If I don't know how to do anything else, I know how to keep myself alive, even when the thought of death by my own hands tried to overwhelm me as an adolescent and young adult. Somehow, without any training or support I would tell myself that the whispers of suicide were not my own, and that I owed it to myself to see what I would become. My favorite scene in *The Color Purple* is the dinner table scene, where the entire family is gathered there with Mister (Celie's abusive husband) on one end and Mister's father at the other end. A family member tells Mister that they will be leaving after dinner and that they will take Celie with them to their home out of state. As customary, Mister begins insulting Celie. We expect that Celie will take it as she always has but she raises her head and her voice is beautiful as she insults him back. "You a low-down dirty dog, that's what's wrong." One can see the adrenaline surging through Celie's body like power and as she eventually stands up and holds a knife to Mister's throat. It is triggering and beautiful for me to witness, as I become tall and strong too. As she leaves, Mister follows her out to the porch threatening to hit her, and she turns around holding two fingers in the air pointing at him as if she could pluck his eyes with them. "Until you do right by me, everything you think about is going to fail." That line is freedom to me. If I am held back from advancing in academia because I am Black, ugly, a woman, or nappy headed, that university too will be held back. Between the oversized dossier, a global shutdown, and worldwide civil unrest, my striving to be seen and acknowledged had ceased. Like Celie said, "I'm poor, Black, I may even be ugly, but dear God, I'm here."

And since I am here, I have finally learned to use my voice

and presence to make sure people know that Black lives matter. I began sitting on faculty search committees with an intention to increase the number of Black faculty from three to ten within my first three years. I knew this invisible labor would be time consuming and painstaking but what good was I if I stayed content to have a seat at the table and not provide chairs for others?

In three years, I sat on seven faculty search committees, chaired the one in my department, and was instrumental in the hiring of seven Black women across the campus! If you're white or low on the Black racial identity development continuum I know what you might be thinking—no, I did not put Black people in place because they were Black, and no, I did not over-rule anyone or coerce the teams of four to six people I worked with. Aside from the spelling of people's names there was no way of knowing the race or ethnicity of candidates. In fact, one of the women whom the psychology department was excited about hiring was named Victoria. I agreed she should be inter-viewed. I was just as surprised as my colleagues to see a Black face on the screen of the virtual meeting space. To increase the number of faculty of color, I simply added "demonstrates evidence of commitment to diversity and inclusion" as part of our selection criteria and had the search committee rank applications as they reviewed teaching philosophies, student evaluations, curriculum vitae, and cover letters. I explained my rationale by using faculty bylaws and the revised mission statement of the university inspired by the Black Lives Matter movement, and I spoke about the importance of representation and the empirical benefits students claim having been taught or mentored by Black faculty. Cue Celie's fingers in the air.

CHAPTER 7

Ain't I a Woman?

I've always loved Sojourner Truth's extemporaneous speech "Aint I a Woman?" The boldness with which she spoke, the examples she used to illustrate her points, the infusion of religion, science, and social justice, and the way she challenged her audience in just a few short minutes makes it fascinating. It is what today's young people call a clapback. I wish I was good at clapping back, being able to give a quick, sharp, and effective response to another person's criticism. Unfortunately, I'd learned early on to keep my mouth closed if I didn't have anything good to say. So I trained myself, especially while I was passing, to think so clearly about what had been said to me that by the time I formulated a response it was futile. I used what I called the sandwich method of feedback—start positively, give the constructive response, and end on a positive note, all while keeping my voice even with a fixed smile on my face. By the time I was done, the receiver walked away thinking I'd given a compliment rather than a reprimand. It was an exhausting process, and I'm still not good at responding to people who are quick-mouthed toward me. I keep a copy of

"Ain't I a Woman?" on my office wall so I can remember that it's okay for me to respond off the cuff and that I don't have to lose myself or my message by appeasing the receiver. I remind myself that I am a woman, and not the angry, Black woman they think I am. This was an essential revelation to me since I was reconciling my racial identity because I recognized there were times where I negotiated my gender identity and that it too needed to be reconciled. It was not uncommon to hear me say things to myself such as, "Gird up your loins like a man," an affirmation that came straight from the patriarchal King James Bible whenever I was faced with a challenging situation. Any other woman might have said that she needed to put on her big girl panties. For whatever reasons, that affirmation has never resonated with me.

Early on in my doctoral education, a white woman professor told me she wanted to conduct a study on the dynamics between white women and Black women. I thought it was an interesting concept but I had no idea what she was talking about since I was passing then. I left her office thinking to myself, *there are no dynamics between white and Black women, we are both women and are on the same team.* But now, with my Blackness intact, and an ability to discern when I am experiencing racial microaggressions and flat-out racism I know exactly what she meant. I have experienced these interesting relationship dynamics between white and Black women. Looking back, I find it interesting that she thought it was important to share it with me, especially since there were times when she used privileges she had a white woman and professor to exacerbate the hierarchical dynamics that existed between us. She should definitely carry out that line of research.

As a Black woman, I am no longer caught unaware when I am presumed incompetent because of my race and gender by people who are racially different from me. Once, I was the third member, and the only Black person, of a search committee at the university where I teach. We were interviewing our first candidate, a white woman, for the vacant position. I prepped the candidate for the process and before ending my talk I assured her that she would not have to follow through with one of the customary steps of the interview. This woman thanked me and then looked at my white counterparts and confirmed with them that the step would not be expected of her. After the interview, I asked my counterparts if they noticed the incident. "Yeah, but it's not what you think. She was just making sure." Responses like this used to make me think I was crazy, hyper-focused on the wrong things, and making mountains out of molehills. I know that my experiences are valid and that there is this dynamic between white and Black women that should be further explored, named, and addressed.

The first time I went out of the country, I flew solo to Budapest to deliver my dissertation research at an international conference. I felt afraid and exhilarated at the same time for being in a place where I could not read or speak the language. I am a French fry addict so I had to go to their McDonald's to have my daily dose. I held all my forints out in the shape of a fan so the cashier could take the money needed to pay for my French fries. Knowing I had a palate limited to fast food and southern home cooked meals, my family feared I'd starve across the country. I challenged myself though and ate delicious dishes like ghoulash and things I could not pronounce like baconös-hagymás pirított cikkburgonyaval, hazi csalamádé val. I wanted to fully experience Hungary so that by the time I delivered my talk, I could do so as a person who was a bit more culturally informed. My talk was attended by people from the Netherlands, Paris, the United Kingdom, and so on. As an ice-breaker I asked them to introduce themselves and tell the rest of us why they chose to attend my training. One woman from the Netherlands said, "I just wanted to hear a Black woman speak." I knew I was outside of my country because no one had ever said that before and I felt honored.

I didn't noticed any bad blood between me and white women until the doctoral program, and only then because my process of becoming Black again had begun. Before then, I had close white women friends who told me I was different from other Black people, and I was cool to be around. Heck, I was a maid of honor at one of their weddings, which to me was a sign that I had gotten into the good graces of white folks as I'd aspired to do. Simply, assimilation keeps one from seeing or feeling the danger and impact of backhanded compliments.

When it was time to enter the job market for faculty po-sitions our professors prepared us as best they could. "Just be yourself," they advised. "They are looking for a *fit*. And remem-ber, you're interviewing them just as much as they are inter-viewing you." It sounded like good advice but after bombing the first five telephone interviews I had been offered being myself, I knew I needed a different strategy. Black people do not readily fit anywhere in the Ivory Tower; if anything, it feels like fitting ourselves into something that was not designed for us, like a T-shirt too small. I needed someone I could talk to about my experiences and to see how I could improve my in-terviewing skills at this level.

I found myself standing in the office doorway of a white male professor who had the reputation among us students as one who didn't give a shit. I'd had him for two classes and admired his laid-back approach. I never found him excited or in a hurry about anything. He did not care one iota about impressing others. If you-get-what-you-see was a person, he embodied it. To me, he was the poster child for white maleness. I'd also observed enough of his interactions with the professor who had a target on my back to know that they didn't like each other. All of this led me to believe that he'd make a great ally. "Will you be my dissertation chair?" I asked him, looking down at the floor expecting to be shot down. "Heck, yeah," he said in a voice that made me wrong about him never getting excited about anything. He didn't flinch one bit when I told him I planned to study the dynamics of power, race, and gender between white supervisors and their Black supervisees. I was most impressed when he nodded approvingly when I told him why, recounting the incident in class when my topic was changed. "Well, that was a display of power, race, and gender, wasn't it?" he quipped.

We were joined at the hip from that day on. He was one of the most affirming white men I knew, reminding me of Dr. Baruth from Appalachian State, but with sharper edges. He came through for me in more ways than one. When his father died during the week I was scheduled to defend my dissertation, I expected that my defense would be postponed, which meant my graduation and my employability would also be postponed. I called him, totally willing to accept the postponement. "Absolutely not," he said. "We've got a dissertation to defend."

His allyship made me chastise myself. I'd spent the majority of my passing life looking for white women allies, thinking that womanhood was a bond that empowered us all to win. Only to find out from a white woman that enmity persisted between us. Let me be clear, I am not saying that white women cannot be true allies for Black women. I can count on one hand the names of white women who have advocated for me. But I can also count on two hands the names of white women whose allyship ended when they felt I was encroaching upon their positions (I invite readers to take a look at Dr. Kecia M. Thomas' work to learn more about the Pet to Threat phenomenon). As a result, I have learned how to choose better. I now know the difference between performative allyship and true allyship, although they are not always easy to differentiate. I massaged the self-berating by acknowledging that most of my opportunities for advancement in the white spaces where I worked had come through many white men, but also a few white women. To her, she was only stating the natural order of things based on seniority, but to me she had operated in superiority. Let me say here that if I were still on the lower end of racial identity development and racially passing, I would have assumed that she was mentoring and coaching me. But, being on the higher end I recognized that this was a race-based act.

After a horrible start to phone and in-person interviews, I applied for a second set of jobs. I was more confident about myself, my Blackness, my research and teaching abilities, and what I wanted by then. I nailed every last one of my job talks by phone and scored on-campus interviews. A search committee chair from an HBCU in North Carolina responded to my thank you email by writing, "I found you to be poised and graceful. Thank you for a great interview."

Around the same time I was invited to a huge public university in Florida and gave an outstanding research and teaching demonstration. I was totally comfortable in my skin as a Black woman at this predominantly white institution, unwilling to negotiate any of my identities—gender, race, religious beliefs, motherhood, or wifedom. I brought everything into the rooms, willing to leave emptyhanded if they weren't a good fit for me. Its students and I had a great time, and I appreciated spending time with their faculty. The campus was beautiful and buzzed with youthful energy and I could see myself being there. During the tour when we walked into the main office, we walked through a hallway of about 30 faculty photos lined up on both sides of the walls. All but one of them were white, an Asian American man who was not present at the time of my interview. Unapologetically I asked, "How will having a Black woman change the dynamics of the work you do here?" The buzz from the fluorescent lights overhead was all that could be heard. I was not bummed when I did not receive a job offer. I wanted and needed to be at a university where folks were woke enough to the idea that hiring a person of color was going to be more than checking off a checkbox for diversity. My experiences as a Black doctoral student were evidence enough that things shift amazingly (albeit painstakingly) when a person of color joins the team. Things an all-white team had not noticed before become as clear as day.

I finally scored a job at a smaller and private university in Florida that I fell in love with and had three weeks to relocate there. One of my new white women colleagues mailed local newspapers and magazines to my home. She texted me the names of local Black churches, and social organizations she thought I might be interested in. She even sent me recommendations of good places to eat. I loved her display of allyship and could not wait to join the department with her and the others.

I haven't always known or embraced the power of being a Black woman, and often I've felt the need to negotiate one or both identities, depending on the occasion. When I walk into a predominantly white space, my gender is not salient, race is. Therefore, I look to see how many other Black people are in the room with me, and often I choose to sit with them or nearby. My gender is usually salient when I'm in a predominantly Black space, and I look to see how many other Black women are present. My race and gender are both salient when I find myself in spaces where the audience is mostly white men, but this is rare. The more integrated and comfortable I become, the less I ask myself how authentic I can be in spaces. I watch other women so I can learn how to take up more space and command attention when I walk into rooms. Although my mother was good at this, she was the type of person who would be heard before she was seen, and I preferred to let my presence be known by my personhood rather than my voice, or the sound of my shoes, or any clanging jewelry.

An incident with my mother from my childhood also challenged my budding womanhood. I was about 11 years old when she and I were walking quite a distance to a family member's house. There had been mostly silence between us until she broke the ice.

"Stop walking like that," Brenda demanded angrily, as we walked along a somewhat busy street. "Like what?" I asked, looking down at my legs, trying to figure out what she was criticizing me for. "Like you catcalling." At my young age, I had no idea what she was talking about. But, to correct my gait I straightened my back and placed one foot in front of the other, concentrating on every step I took. *Left...left...left, right, left*. I repeated the drill my step team sergeant used to shout as he had instructed a group of us at-risk kids at the community recreation center, preparing us to perform in the annual Charlotte Thanksgiving Parade. Since Brenda didn't say anything else to me until we reached our destination, I supposed I was walking correctly.

As an adult, I understand her admonishment. Considering society's and the media's hypersexual portrayal of Black girls and women, I suppose that she was trying to protect me. Perhaps she was attempting to make sure I presented as age-appropriate, or keeping me from being predator bait. It probably hinged upon the guilt and powerlessness she might have felt from not being able to protect me from not one but two sexual predators I'd already encountered. So, if telling me to walk straight was her way of protecting me from subsequent assaults then I suppose that she would use whatever power she had, if any, to do so.

Unfortunately for me, I permitted it to be a chink in the armor of my femininity, as I added walk straight to the list of things I could and couldn't do as a Black girl. "Stop walking like that" meant don't draw attention to yourself, don't be desirable, and don't be sexy. To me, Black women are the sexiest beings on the planet. We can't not be sexy. That sway in the hips that Dr. Maya Angelou wrote about in her "Phenomenal Woman" poem is a real thing. The rhythm of my hips cannot be silenced. I tried.

The way I see it, there should be nothing *sexy* to a man or any predator about a young girl, and the onus of protecting her virtue shouldn't be on the child but is the responsibility of the adults and perverts around them. That walk with my mother could have been more fruitful if it had not been filled with silence and shame. It could have been a perfect opportunity to talk about what I presume were her fears, and it could have been used to help shape and build my budding womanhood rather than leaving it open for the world to further tear down.

The world tears down Black girls' and women's femininity by its refusal to see, acknowledge, and uphold their value. It is not hard to see that white girls and women are America's most prized possession. Young white girls can be free, walk as they wish, wear booty shorts, and sashay in heeled shoes even, and it is normalized. When one of them is missing, an all points bulletin is released to enable them to be found. Their family members are given televised opportunities to plead for assistance. A whopping 38 percent of the people who are reported missing in the US are Black, more than double the around 14 percent of the population who are Black, according to the Black and Missing Foundation. Yet, when Black girls and women are murdered or missing, there is a national silence and victim blaming.

When Gabby Petito went missing, the video of her being interviewed by the police during a traffic stop played nonstop on our televisions. We were shown that she was traveling the country with an abusive boyfriend; still nobody blamed her for being with a man who later murdered her. Instead, the world wondered what it could have done differently to save her. When Breona Taylor was murdered by the police, she was blamed posthumously for having had a relationship with a man whose alleged criminal lifestyle brough the police to her doorstep.

Black people have enough experience to know that we will receive little to no help, and with time being a critical factor in successfully finding our missing daughters, sisters, or friends, we mobilize ourselves through social media, using Black Twitter and Facebook to fight for justice for our girls and women. It is shameful, albeit powerful, that we have had to set up our own organizations to find missing Black women and girls. I applaud grassroot organizations such as Blackandmissing.com and the social media group Missing Black Women and Girls. I salute Minnesota's Office of Missing and Murdered African American Women, and the state of California for being the first to establish the Ebony Alert, a public alert that is activated when Black children and women go missing. These efforts are encouraging as we fight to get them instituted nationally.

The world chips away at Black women's femininity through music, movies, and on television, and sometimes by creators who look like us. I looked for women on television to pattern myself after but there were not many dark-skinned women shown when I was growing up—heck, there weren't many Black women on TV at all. I didn't like black-and-white shows, so I missed Diahann Carroll and Eartha Kitt, and I did not like Blaxploitation films so I didn't see Pam Grier. I watched *The Jeffersons* and *Good Times* and was inspired by Weezy and her friend Helen, both of whom were beautiful Black women. I would become an adult before I came to appreciate Esther Rolle's beauty. I understood that Black women were progressing on television from mammies, to jezebels, to crack queens, to dope dealers, with inadvertent messages that we were unattractive and unmarriable. Phylicia Rashad acting as Claire Huxtable changed the game for me. Seeing a depiction that meant I could be beautiful, have a high-paying job, marry a successful Black man, and could have five children—a number that made people look at Black women as welfare queens—was inspiring and I can't readily think of another show with such a message. Later we would be inundated with shows, with *Girlfriends*, *Living Single*, and *All of Us* drilling home the message that Black women are unmarriable and should focus on being happy as single and divorced women.

If I couldn't get a positive portrayal of who I should or could be as a Black woman from my family, or television, or music, then I imagine that white people's interpretations of those portrayals could be worse than mine. And don't tell me white people are not informed by television because during one of my diversity trainings to a predominantly white audience I asked them to guess the kind of music the person next to them listened to, and I gave them options of music (country, rap, gospel, blues, jazz, pop, and so on). We went around the room so the audience could share their answers. We asked their neighbors if the answer was correct, and we asked what led the person to choose that music genre for their neighbor. This is definitely an activity to bring biases and assumptions to one's awareness. One person said she chose alternative music for her neighbor based on the way she dressed—an outfit that could be considered earthy. A white man got his music choice wrong for the full-figured Black woman beside him. Her music choice was rap and he had chosen gospel. When asked why, he said, "I used to love *Gimme a Break!* when I was growing up, and she reminded me of Nell Carter. I think of all Black women as nice and nurturing. So, I picked gospel."

Just as I know the transgenerational impact of post-slavery on Black people, I am not naive enough to believe that post-colonialism does not run through white people's veins. I am not saying that all Black people are subservient to white people, just as I'm not saying that all white people are racist. What I am saying is that racism was not eradicated by laws, legislation, and the election of a Black president. It grew up with us, became more mature and sophisticated. It may not lynch, or burn down businesses and communities but it redlines, gerrymanders, passes discriminatory legislation, gatekeeps, and entraps. Just as some Black people live with DNA altered by the lashes from slave owners on their bodies, and the selling and separation of family members, and from watching their loved ones being lynched, white people live with the DNA of having administered the lashings, the power of owning people as property, and from watching the lynchings with their families.

I have come to know the power of white women. Dr. Stephanie E. Jones-Rogers' research called our attention to the overlooked role of women slave owners. Her findings indicate that over 40 percent of slave owners were white women. Right before that, I'd read *Never Caught*, Erica Armstrong Dunbar's retelling of Ona Judge Staines' defiant escape from the first US president George Washington and his wife Martha. Martha was the one who increased the number of enslaved on their property. On his deathbed, George had the courage to override Martha and deem Ona and others to be free people. I wonder how the superiority and power among white women from the past contribute to the phenomenon of "Karenism," where white women take it upon themselves to oversee the actions of Black people.

The collective power of white women is mesmerizing to me. It can be witnessed by their efforts to reform the eugenics project. Forced sterilizations occurred in other countries to prevent births of people who lived with intellectual disabilities, in order to have a fit society. Being able to control a population by ensuring that it is fit seemed ideal to the US. Soon, the US broadened the definition of fit to include race and socioeconomic status. Poor Black women were sterilized, often without consent, more than any other race or gender. The Eugenics Project ended around 1972. Margaret Sanger's idea for reform was Planned Parenthood, a more ethical way to control unwanted pregnancies. Today, there are over 600 clinics, which is great news since this helps women take responsibility for their own bodies. The horrible news is that 80 percent of the clinics are in Black communities, which is not reformative at all.

To many Americans' surprise, a large percentage of white women voted for President Trump when he was elected, despite claims of misogyny. If the link between Dr. Jones-Rogers' work and white women's votes for Trump had been widely understood, it might have lessened the shock.

The power of white women could be evidenced by the one white woman who successfully removed prayer from schools. Money allocated for women- and minority-owned businesses and COVID-based emergency business loans goes to white women more than to any other demographic. And the counseling profession of which I am a part is comprised of 70 percent white counselors, 73.3 percent of whom are white women.

When there is this much homogeneity and hierarchy, there is much power and gatekeeping.

I would be remiss if I did not mention, however, the positive and good work that this group produces. The collective power of white women took breast cancer under its wing and the Susan G. Komen Foundation, one of the largest funded nonprofits there is, was created.

I was mindful of this power when I considered applying to be the chair of our department at the university where I work. Though not in academia, I had varied program development experience and knew I could take our department to a higher level and extend our visibility nationally. After consulting with other women who were chairs and deans, I knew I could do an amazing job even if it would be an initial learning curve. However, I sensed that our department was not ready for a Black woman in leadership, especially since there were none in leadership across the campus. I'd also sensed that my being a candidate might disrupt the cohesion we shared, especially considering that there were co-workers who had seniority over me. Eventually, I talked myself out of applying but that did not stop the woman who I considered an ally putting me in my place during the faculty meeting where she announced her candidacy. She did a great job outlining her qualifications and I snapped my fingers for her. I didn't grow cold until she ended with, "Now if LaTonya wants to be chair, she can serve after me...." To her, she was only stating the natural order of things based on seniority, but to me she had operated in superiority. I felt affirmed when one of our newer faculty members, a Black woman, cornered me after the meeting and said, "That was some bullshit. The biggest display of privilege I have ever seen." After sitting with feelings of anger, disappointment, and betrayal for a couple of weeks, I went to my newly appointed chair and initiated a conversation about the incident and asked for support to repair the rupture that had occurred between us. It has been over a year and we are still working through the ups and down of restoration.

I love the solidarity I get from associating with Black women. I belong to collectives of them knowing that we can do more together than alone. I look forward to us using our power in the same ways white women do. People think that Black women don't get along, and that we cannot be in a room together for long without a fight breaking out, and that we have crab-in-a-barrel syndrome, where we knock each other down to move upward. Those are not the Black women I attract. I wouldn't be where I am without the three beautiful sisters I call my best friends. We helped raise each other's children when we were single mothers. We pooled our money together when any of us was in need. We paid each other's bills when one of us couldn't. When one of us had, we all had. Recently, I was on a video call with a Black woman colleague from another university, supporting her while she prepared for tenure and promotion. I spoke about anticipatory trouble with my process and said, "Naw sis, you got a nation full of sisters who will show up for you."

I also long for white and Black women to come together, and that feminism and womanism will collide and that equity will be birthed from the collision. I have had very many positive experiences with white women that counterbalance the negative ones. Dr. Geri Miller, a former professor of mine at Appalachian State University, was one of the first to take me under her wing. Her invitation to speak at a national conference was the beginning of my identity as a scholar, nearly 20 years after our first encounter. Dr. Kate Brinko, another former professor and supervisor, perfected my written communication skills and loved my firstborn child like her own when I worked for her as a young mother. Dr. Laurie Garo, a professor who was not an instructor of mine, made herself and her two daughters the firstborn's official babysitters.

I work with white women colleagues whom I adore and when ruptures take place in our relationships, I work with them for resolution. This type of maturity is required from both parties if white and Black women are going to improve the divide between us. I await the day when Black women no longer have to prove our worth, partake in respectability politics, ask or fight for economic equity, or remind the powers-that-be that we too are women.

Part 3
LIVING AND LOVING MYSELF

CHAPTER 8

Close, But Far

"If one or both of your parents graduated from college, take one step forward," I say loudly to the newest class of students in my master's level Ethics and Legal Considerations in Counseling course. We are on campus outside in the parking lot of our two-year-old two-story brick building, standing in Jacksonville's humid evening heat, and the students are lined up horizontally across the smooth black pavement. I watch most of the white students break line and step forward and I notice that the four students of color—an Ethiopian woman and three Black women—stand stiffly in place. I catch a glimpse of a white woman student swat a bug from near her face, "I hate Florida's bugs," she proclaims with an effectively timed comic relief from the tension and heat.

I look at the other 14 statements I will read from an activity known as The Privilege Walk, often used to demonstrate the impact of privilege and oppression, and for self-awareness. "If you knew since you were a child that it was expected of you to go to college, take one step forward." I observe almost all the students move on a step.

I began the next statement slowly and deliberately so all could hear. "If there have been times in your life when you skipped a meal because there was no food in the house, take one step backward." The students who stepped backward were back at the starting line. And the next question would put them back a step further: "If you were ever stopped by the police because they felt you were suspicious, take one step backward." I skipped down two questions to give them some breathing room, and I watched them exhale as they stepped forward on, "If there were more than 50 books in your house growing up, take one step forward."

After the fifteenth question, I surveyed the line. It was our first class and they did not know me aside from what they had read online, and I had not yet learned their names, so I was not able to call on students specifically. To all of them I offered, "Using one word, describe how you feel right now, and feel free to explain your answer." *Guilty. Sad. Not surprised. Sober. Aware.* I asked the students at the front of the line, who were a five-row distance from the students in the very back, to describe how it felt to be at the front of the line. Both white male students said that it didn't matter to them, and that neither one of them was surprised. The white woman student on the line with them mentioned that she felt guilty, having started out with everyone, and then moving forward while watching people fall behind. I asked the students in the last row, mostly students of color, how it felt to be back there, and they too said that they weren't surprised. One noted that once they got the hang of the questions, they knew where their positions would be. Some of the students in the middle were surprised; most thought they would be further ahead and a couple of them thought they would have been further behind. Then, I led a discussion to process the questions, asking if there were some more than others that were surprising to them. One student reported that she lied by not moving forward on questions because she did not want her peers to think that she thought she was better than they were. Another student was able to point out that that too was a privilege. One of the front-row male students offered that, "If you had used another set of questions, I guarantee that I would not be on the front row," unknowingly showing that being on the front row did matter to him.

Subscribing to a multicultural framework of pedagogy, I explained that none of the rows—front, middle, or back—was bad. The point of the activity was to be aware of one's privilege—and we all have privilege—and the opportunity to use the power we have to empower others. I also shared my experiences when I'd taken The Privilege Walk with others. I, too, was in the very back row each time, even when different questions were asked. One time, a question was asked about golf, that if I or my parents played golf then I could take one step forward. Of course, I didn't step forward. But, if they had asked if my parents or I played Spades, I would have been able to. I shared that *anger* was the word that captured how I felt and still feel. I'd pursued education through the lens of Horace Mann's 1848 proclamation that education was *the great equalizer*. "Yet I have the highest degree in the land and am still rows behind my white counterparts who have the same or less experience than I do."

The front-row student raised his hand again, and when I acknowledged him he said, "But, shouldn't you just be grateful that you have a doctorate degree and can sit among them?" I think it was the "just be grateful" part that made me want to clap back. I had two things in the forefront of my mind: I could not lose my audience for one person, and none of the students knew me well enough to know I wouldn't intentionally mean harm. But I also believed that there would be other students who would also see his response as insensitive and privileged. I couldn't have created a better teaching moment by myself. "Class, this is a perfect example from someone who stands at the front of the line. Often, people with the most privilege are not aware of its impact on others. Only a person at the front of the line would ask me to *just be grateful*. I wonder how someone at the middle or back of the line might respond to what I shared." A woman at the back raised her hand, "Your comment resonated with me," she shared. "No matter how close I get to success, I still feel so far from it."

That student summed up the totality of my existence up to that point in one sentence. I had been so busy running from my past and striving for an opposite future, that I was not living. I was simply moving from task to task, with accomplishments as milestones but not much celebration in between. A nearly three-year pandemic helped me see that I wasn't living at all. When I wasn't drowning, I was holding my breath. When work cut out or slowed down during the pandemic, I was left to examine if I was using my life force the way I really wanted to use it or if I was simply doing what I thought I ought to be doing. At this point in my racial identity development I was able to be Black and explore other areas of life outside race and gender. Who else was I in addition to womanness and Blackness? I challenged myself to make the exploration fun.

There were a few things I wanted to experiment with anyway. I wanted to explore the softer side of myself and play—two things I didn't have much experience with. I hired a Black woman mental health therapist who could help me talk through barriers when they arose and hold me accountable. First, we identified what softness meant to and for me. The simple act of saying I wanted to be softer was not easy. Culturally and familially, being soft meant being weak, a crier, not able to handle much, a target, and one could easily be hurt. I did not want to be any of those things I used to be as a child. I trained myself to be hard, exteriorly, and psychologically, emotionally, and mentally.

I no longer wanted to be regimented, rigid, calculated, predictable, and literal. I was able to recognize that those characteristics were responses I'd developed to create a sense of safety and control to counterbalance the trauma I'd endured. Those same characteristics also helped me navigate through predominately white spaces, as they had done for my ancestors during slavery and Jim Crow. Having a hard personality meant I took everything seriously and I played the part with my attire and affect. However, it was exhausting and I wanted to laugh more and be lighter. I wanted to be free.

I surprised myself when I walked into a pawn shop looking for a keyboard. There is not a musical bone in my body but I love piano and organ music and I wanted to experiment with something that would take time to learn. My personality means that I walk into a store and know exactly what I am looking for, size it up, buy it, and leave. But, to learn how to live, my therapist challenged me to savor moments, to slow down to fully experience them, and to use all of my senses. If I were not a therapist myself I would have left her office thinking she was the one who needed help, talking about making sure I notice what I smell, see, hear, feel, and taste. As a survivalist, I heavily relied on my senses to inform me of danger. I could read body language like a prosecutor, hear what people were really telling me even though they were saying something else, and I could feel in my gut when something was not quite right. This contributed to my avoidance of large crowds, and I don't shop or go to banks first thing in the morning, at lunchtime, or right after work when there are usually more people there.

But this time, walking in to the pawn shop I exhaled and took deep breaths while I explored items. I made my way to the musical instruments where there was everything but a keyboard. I noticed a Mitchell guitar that someone had hand-painted with a woman standing against a backdrop of greenery and flowers. I surmised that it belonged to a creative soul who loved it and might come back for it. It cost $129 and I figured for that price I could buy a brand-new guitar. Before I could talk myself out of it, I went to a nearby guitar store and bought an acoustic Mitchell that I named Mahogany. The giddy feeling in my heart and head were so unfamiliar I wondered if I was in a midlife crisis. But, I could not stop smiling.

"You're going to love this guitar," the cashier told me after learning I was a beginner. "If you play through the pain, you're going to be fine."

I thought he was talking about emotional pain, as in Roberta Flack's *Killing Me Softly*. I had lots of emotional pain I needed to strum out on Mahogany. I came to find out that he was talking about real physical pain! Playing guitar hurts like crap. The constant pressing down on the fret board and guitar strings with my fingertips felt like grabbing hold of a sticker briar bush over and over again. While talking to others about my new passion, I learned that one of my neighbors and a colleague were guitar players. They both warned me about the pain and told me to practice long enough to get callouses and then the pain would stop. "Show me your callouses when they come in," one of them offered.

That was a revelation to me. Wait, I'm supposed to let myself hurt long enough to develop a defense against it? How profound. All of these years I have been running from pain, and here I had been just invited to embrace it. If only I had known that might apply to my own emotional pain, I wouldn't have run from it. I wouldn't have dropped Blackness thinking that whiteness was a panacea. Pain wasn't a sign to stop or that I was doing something wrong. It was required and celebrated as evidence of growth.

I wanted to share this revelation with the world. Sure, I could tweet it or post it but I wondered if there was a more captive audience. I wondered if there was a local TEDx Talk event. I googled it and found that I had eight days to apply. *Don't even think about it*, I thought to myself as I logged off the website. There is no way you can craft a message in eight days. I went for a walk around the community to rid myself of the frenetic energy I felt coursing through my body. *If I could deliver a message to the world about pain in eight minutes, what would I say?* I asked myself, walking like a mad woman past my neighbors' houses. I started thinking about the impact of COVID on myself and many of the people I knew, and how badly we could use an inspirational message. By the time I got back home two miles later, I had a tentative outline of my talk. I submitted *Know Pain, Know Gain*, and weeks later I received an invitation to share the message on the TEDx Jacksonville's stage.

"You need to put your ass out the window," Yvette, my TEDx Talk coach told me. "You gave this whole talk and you're not even in it. We don't see you. What's your story? What qualifies you to tell other people what to do with their pain when you won't share yours?"

I narrowed my eyes at her. All of the other coaches who spoke before her had either nodded their heads in approval of my talk, or had great things to say about me, my delivery of it, and the talk itself. But here she was, the only Black coach on the staff, with plenty to say about what I didn't do and what she couldn't see. However, at this point of my life I had come to embrace opportunities for growth and life had expanded beyond the lines of race and gender, Black and white.

I looked at the pages of my talk, a whole eight minutes about my 25 years as a mental health therapist and how I'd helped others work through their pain. I even had an acronym for HURT that my audience could use to overcome emotional pain that kept them from living, or wanting to live.

"We don't care about the work you've done with others. We want to know how you got over your pain," Yvette offered.

For a brief moment, I considered dropping out. First, I didn't have time to rewrite a whole talk when the event was just a few weeks away and I had a job and family I needed to tend to after work. Then, there was my appointed coach, a white woman whose career as a speaking coach and actress led her to tell me that I was telling too much and needed to cut out parts of the talk, while the Black coach believed I wasn't telling enough. It was all confusing, exhausting, not to mention we were not being paid for our time or our talks. "My children don't even know my story," I heard myself say to the panel of coaches. "There's no way I'm going to get on a national stage and talk about my life. I would like to present my talk the way I proposed when you accepted it."

I couldn't sleep for the angst associated with knowing Yvette was right. I searched my heart for an eight-minute message I felt comfortable sharing, and then called my children. "You guys know I have been selected to give a TEDx Talk," I paused as they cheered. "But what you don't know is the life story I've been asked to share." I rehearsed my talk with them, and listened to their silence as I put meat on the bones of skeletal phrases I had always given them during their upbringing like, "I was adopted," "Me and your dad grew apart," and, "My childhood wasn't the best."

The firstborn might have been the first to break silence with a "Wow." I lightened the mood with, "I know, right?" Then I asked if they had any questions, comments, or thoughts, quickly falling back on the comfort of the professoriate in the way I handle students during my lectures.

"I'm proud of you," the middle child said. "The world needs to hear that. That's going to help a lot of people." The baby girl, who is adopted like I am, was the quietest, but she did say she couldn't wait to see it live.

Practices for the TEDx Talk event were painful for me. Not only because I was honing my talk—cutting and adding, putting my ass out there a little more each week because Yvette would say I was still hiding, but also because I am introverted and I hate being front and center. On top of that I am clumsy, and the coaches told us we needed to use our arms and body, for genuineness and credibility, and we needed to use the stage by moving from center stage to left stage, back to center, then to right and back to center as we talked. I literally can only do one thing at a time, so I knew my talk was going to go one of two ways: I was either going to forget my lines while remembering to move left and right, or I was going to trip over the signature red TEDx Talk carpet. There was a third option: that I would die from a panic attack.

I messed up my lines so many times before the event that when the day finally arrived, I was sick of my coaches, my talk, and myself. I wanted nothing more than to be done. My sleep had been interrupted too many times by my opening line begging for attention. *If I had known then what I know now...* The speakers and I received our last set of instructions. "Just remember," the TEDx Jacksonville organizer warned, "the audience out there isn't your real audience. Your real audience is made up of the folks across the country who will watch your recording." Panic set in again and intensified after each speaker before me returned to the green room after their performance. I was speaker number five, after the intermission. Speakers exited the stage and made a beeline for the green room, where we cheered, congratulated, and cried with them as they absorbed the feeling of delivering an error-free talk and that they'd just completed one of the biggest talks of their lives.

Finally, it was my turn. My stomach was tight, and my breath felt caught in my throat, as if I might vomit or hyperventilate. I kept both at bay by taking deep breaths, because my family and friends were in that front row and online and they were waiting for me, praying for me. So, even if it killed me, I was going to get on that stage and get the contents of my speech out of my head and spirit. *Just have fun*, I told myself.

As instructed, I did not walk out until my name appeared on the projected screen. Oddly, I waved to the audience as I approached them. Delivering the talk was surreal, especially since I could not fully connect to myself. After enduring so many traumatic events, the one thing my body does well when it perceives that I am in trouble is separate from my mind so there is less impact. On stage, I was watching myself give the talk, feeding myself lines, and reminding my body to move from right to center to left. I was numb, I didn't feel anything. The overhead lights helped as I could barely see the audience members' faces. I knew I was disconnected, and by the time I got to the last paragraph of my talk my mind went blank. My head bowed in shame and a breath of despair escaped my womb, but then the lines came. The ending, where I was sup-posed to *knock 'em dead*, was delivered quickly before I could forget the words. The crowd cheered, and as they began stand-ing, I bowed and exited swiftly, unable to accept what I inter-preted as their praise or pity.

My fellow speakers cheered and congratulated me as I had done them. One of them held my face in her hands, "You fuck-ing killed it," she said with her teeth clenched tight, for em-phasis. Moments later, the organizer entered the green room, "You got the first full standing ovation of the evening," she exclaimed.

My natural inclination is not to believe people, espe-cially when they deliver good news. I understand that now as a trauma response. Condemnation feels more like home than praise does. Praise feels like a foreign language. I do not understand it. I am not fluent, or even conversant in it. But, I'm working on myself. I had to tell my brain to use my senses to fully experience the moment. I still heard the cheer from the audience. I listened to my fellow speakers tell me how they experienced my talk. I felt some of their hands on my shoulders, others on my back, and one pair clasping mine. I forced myself to not turn away from their eye contact. I tasted newness and discomfort, and swallowed them both. I felt shaky from having completed it all but I was friggin' proud of myself. I had just told the world to process pain advantageously, because the level of their pain is indicative of the level of their greatness. And I believed myself.

Since the talk, I have continued to explore ways to be softer, or more *vulnerable*, as I have come to know this as another word for soft. There was no room for vulnerability in my childhood or in my assimilation to whiteness. Much like the traditional form of passing, where fair-skinned people of color presented and were accepted as white people, and there was great angst and much care taken to mask speech, to stay out of the sun, and so on, I too felt like vulnerability might get me killed.

I had no idea how closely related vulnerability is to honesty. I always prided myself on being a person of integrity, a person whom people could trust. But my therapist skillfully pointed out that assimilation—the act of acquiring things that are not my own and hiding myself to keep them—is not honesty. I thought of integrity in terms of not intentionally lying, not stealing, and not talking about others behind their back—stuff like that—but I came to learn that for me dishonesty was also rooted in people-pleasing, perfectionism, and passivity.

Doing things for others when I didn't want to and giving

to them what I wanted to keep was an automatic response for me. Not permitting myself to make mistakes or give myself the grace to learn and grow were also ways that stunted my ability to be authentic and be true to myself. Accepting what others gave me without setting expectations or boundaries was another way I denied myself. Since these behaviors were developed in my childhood and perfected while assimilating, undoing them might be a lifelong process for me.

There are many ways I have come to practice vulnerability. Besides reclaiming my weekends for fun and living (I put up an out-of-office message on all of my email accounts Friday through Sunday), I do my best to speak what I think *and* feel, permit myself to cry when my body signals that crying is the way it wants to relieve tension, and try new foods and new routes when I go to the same places. Two acts of vulnerability that have been much harder for me to practice are asking for help and working with others. In childhood, I learned to not ask for help because I saw that people were struggling themselves and could not help me, or there were times when people didn't help me, and there were times when I asked for help but didn't ask the right people. I just learned to take care of myself. By the time I arrived at assimilating, I didn't ask for help because I worked hard against stereotype threat. People who succumb to stereotype threat do things to prove that the stereotype is not real. Because I loathe hearing people say Colored People Time, or CPT, where they subscribe to the belief that Black people are always late, I am always on time. I can be fighting mad when I'm in a meeting with white people but nobody would know, as a smile would be plastered across my face and my voice would be even. They would not have the pleasure of calling me an angry Black woman. So not asking for help while assimilating meant I would not perpetuate the stereotype that Black people are lazy or unintelligent, or had only gotten in the door due to affirmative action.

Being the only Black person in many white spaces, I didn't want to give the impression that I did not belong there, that I was a token, or that I was going to steal or take anything from them. So, I figured things out for myself, which meant I over-worked and outworked. Asking for help still feels like incompetence to me, but I continue to have to rework and reframe the messages I received while growing up. I heard things like, *If you want something done right then do it yourself.* Or, *By the time I tell or show you what I need I could have done it myself.* I do believe that when I learn to ask the right people for help and trust people I'm working with, I meet success as I've imagined it, which means I am freed up to live. I am freed up to do more and have more. Plus, I deserve to learn and grow and I deserve to have help.

Vulnerability may mean different things to different people, but for me one last way to be vulnerable (at least it's last at this point in my recovery) is the ability to say no. I do recognize that in areas of my life where I am rigid, saying yes more is an act of vulnerability. For example, I rarely say yes to last-minute invitations. I need at least a week or two to mentally prepare myself to do something outside of my routine. Reflecting on it here makes me realize that being that controlled has hindered my ability to live freely. For me, it has been about providing protection and safety for myself since I didn't have access to them as a child. But I realize I can practice living fearlessly by saying no to indiscriminate requests for meetings, money, and so on.

Faulty thinking stemming from childhood and assimilation issues kept me putting others' needs before my own, which meant my calendar was full while my bank account was not. I do not know why I cannot say no to a request when I can fulfill it. Like if someone asks me for money and I have the dollar amount in my account, I cannot say no. Or, if they need a place to stay or to borrow my car, I say yes even when I do not want to. Perhaps, I am still bound by the it is better to give than receive bullcrap, or if I give it will be given unto me, or the dozens of other scriptures I was taught to use to sacrifice myself. Honestly, I know it's my past. Since I know what it's like to be homeless, to not have my basic needs met, and to depend on people who did not come through for me, it makes it hard for me to let other people feel pain. But what is more honest about my inability to say no is feelings of guilt. I have to force myself to not feel guilty about making it out of a life of lack and destruction. I have to permit others to stay there and not feel obligated to pull everybody out with me, especially when some of them do not want to leave.

A response I am practicing until it becomes a second-nature response others who make requests I do not want to fulfill is, "I'm sorry I am not able to do that." The "not able" does not have to mean that I can't, it needs to mean that psychologically I am not able to fulfill the request. The psychological process I go through after I give up something I wanted to keep is more painful for me than the act of giving the thing.

Interestingly, being Black again has bridged the gap between where I am and where I want to be. I no longer feel far from arriving at the space I see in my spirit where I shall dwell, partly because I no longer claim what people call imposter syndrome—defined as feelings of self-doubt and fraudulence. When I learned that the term was coined by two white women who survey mostly white executive-level women, I knew it didn't apply to me. How could findings be generalized to people of color? I chose not to label or punish myself for daring to dream or go farther. Feelings of nervousness or not-yet-knowing should be normalized when you get to a space you're new to. If anyone ought to feel like a fraud, it's the people who already occupy the space and feel uncomfortable when I arrive. It reminds me of drapetomania, a race-based disease theorized by Dr. Samuel Cartwright of the early 1900s characterized by an uncontrollable or insane compulsion to wander, ascribed to enslaved people who tried to run for their freedom. The enslaved were punished for dreaming, wanting more, desiring freedom. So no, people like me who want better lives aren't imposters, the ones who keep us from it are. Finding my own way has been freeing in itself and has led me to be a more loving person toward myself and others.

CHAPTER 9
On Loving

I found out the hard way that assimilation, my striving toward white ways of living, was a demonstration of self-hatred. I thought it was the ultimate act of self-love, grabbing a hold of things not readily accessible to me and using them to get ahead. I did not know that whiteness was out of reach for a reason. Who knew that the adage was true, that one truly cannot serve two masters. The more love I gained for whiteness, the more hatred I developed toward my Black self. Unfortunately, I did not recognize the signs of self-hatred because I thought hating oneself looked like cutting, excessive drinking and drug use, promiscuity, suicidal behaviors, and not taking care of oneself. Not many of those were applicable to me. Looking back, I can clearly see self-condemnation in other ways, beginning with how I defined love.

Either I've been all wrong about love, or its meaning is as fluid as I have been. As my youngest self, I thought love was an action. I knew I was loved or cared for or safe by what another person did for me, or by the way they spoke to and about me. As I grew into a teenager, I conceptualized love as a feeling. I identified it by what I felt in my heart and believed that it felt like fluttering butterflies in my stomach. As a young adult, and a self-righteous Christian by then, I surmised love to be synonymous with integrity. To me, love was evidenced by a person doing what they said they were going to do, and I assessed it by the congruency of their words and actions. Now, love to me is maturity, not a feeling or action but a sense of being able to take the good and the bad and to extend grace to myself and others when needed.

For a long time, I blamed Brenda and Brother Ali for my inability to love, find love, or be lovable. Brenda's sternness and Brother Ali's absence showed up in my relationships in a lot of ways. From the blueprint on love I'd been handed, my sternness manifested as independence and control and attracted partners who were physically present but emotionally absent, or emotionally present and physically absent. My parents had been great practicing grounds for my choosing to be in relationships with partners who were abusive, addicted, or absent. I had mastered loyalty and long-suffering by holding out for hope in parents who were not able to show love for me in healthy ways. I thought that loyalty and self-sacrifice were the keys to love and I thought they were qualities that made me lovable.

I was much older and in therapy and administering therapy to clients like myself when I resolved that Brenda and Brother Ali's only assignment in my life was to get me here on earth. Accepting that their assignment had been completed permitted me to absolve them of any other responsibility, and actually helped me to feel grateful toward them. I recognized that they could have chosen differently and aborted me, or worse. I accepted that the responsibility to create a good life for me was not theirs but mine. I initially may have chosen a harmful path by believing that a better life meant living by white standards, but I was able to extend grace to myself by acknowledging that at least I did something. I did not stay stuck. I did not stay resentful. I did not continue passing, nor did I stay afraid of myself or my people. And I did not end up like the statistics predicted that I would—an abuser, on drugs, in jail, or dead.

Learning to love myself and finding myself lovable has been an interesting journey. Early in the journey, I happened upon Louise Hay's book, *You Can Heal Your Life*. Hay's premise is that much of our malaise is due to self-lovelessness. I love that the author challenged her readers to explore childhood messages and behaviors and to positively reframe them in adulthood. She ended each chapter with affirmations and exercises like mirror work, which simply put is an activity where readers practice becoming comfortable enough with themselves to look intently into their eyes in the mirror and repeat affirmations until the day comes when they believe them. Trust me when I tell you that this is easier said than done but it is worthwhile in disrupting core beliefs. I had many core beliefs associated with Blackness, poverty, physical appearance, and self-worth to disintegrate, and Hay's book helped me identify affirmations to better articulate how to talk to and about myself. I return to the book every couple of years to redo the work. That book, and the many other self-help books I've read—bibliotherapy as we therapists call it: the healing through books—is a very affordable and accessible precursor and supplement to therapy and has taught me to love myself.

While learning to love myself, one of my adulthood best friends led me to assess my wardrobe for its effectiveness as an expression of self-love. When I met April, I dressed in clothing that was black, brown, beige, and navy. This is partly because, as a dark-skinned woman, I had been taught not to wear bright colors and I hated pastels, and also because as a sexual abuse survivor I had learned not to draw attention to myself. April was a fair-skinned woman who was always dressed fabulously, with perfectly styled hair and makeup, so it took her a lot to convince me that I could be fabulous too. I conceded when my publisher sent me on a national tour to promote the novel that I had written, *Good To Me*, in the early 2000s and I commissioned April to "style" me. I am not kidding when I write that bookstores sold out of my books every time I wore the bright red, crushed velvet jacket April bought for me to wear book signings. My book sales went through the roof as I traveled with the clothing April had come up with—her boldest choice was a turquoise, rust, and beige paisley corduroy jacket with a pair of turquoise corduroy pants to match. I came to love color against my dark chocolate skin and I eventually quit protesting when April made sure my makeup popped with color, too. Before her makeup artistry, I was content with clear lip gloss and translucent powder on my face, but April had me wearing gold and silver eyeshadows and red, burgundy, and fuchsia lipsticks—things I would never have chosen for myself. It is now years later and I have not gone back to wearing muted colors on my face or body, especially now as a full-bodied Black woman who understands the power and influence that comes from being such.

Recently, I felt the urge to assess my wardrobe again as I wanted to see what it reflected about me. More honestly, I was feeling some angst about turning 50 years old and I wanted to see what my closet would reveal—would it show youthfulness or aging? Would it show room for growth or the stuckness I felt? I love opening the doors of my closet and being met with vibrant greens, yellows, pinks, and so on, and various patterns of stripes, blocks, and paisley, animal-like prints of cheetah, leopard, and dalmatian, and Afrocentric printed skirts and dresses. Interestingly, though, I found a blaring limitation that I had not been aware of. My closet only housed two kinds of clothing and shoes—work and church attire. What a sad revelation. It was indicative of the fact that I had no night life, no life outside work, and I showed little attention toward myself as a person outside the professoriate and church. Reflecting on this led to an acknowledgement that I needed and wanted a life at 50 years old and a wardrobe to wear it to. I made an intention to live more and to add jeans and shorts, casual tops and flat shoes so I could. It's so not my personality to wear shiny stuff but lately—and I'm going to blame it on getting older—I've been wanting a sequined blouse. I have no idea where I would wear it, but it will be an act of self-love to purchase it and find a reason to wear it.

It is important for me to say that I do not believe that self-love and self-care cost money. Massages, nail and hair care, retreats and vacations, and outings are nice but I have done all of these things and still felt lonely, unloved, and worn out. I have come to subscribe to what Black womanists call radical self-care, whereby taking care of and showing love for oneself is conducted by saying no to people, places, and things that are no longer mutually beneficial. I do this by paying attention to my gut because my head will have me automatically saying yes to requests without considering whether I have the financial, psychological, or spiritual capacity to carry them out. But my gut—the innermost part of me, the pit of my stomach, the part of myself I call spirit or wisdom—will churn or flip from conviction when I say yes to something I know I should walk away from. Self-love is listening to and honoring what I discern.

This is important to those who are recovering from assimilating or passing. When looking at ourselves through the white gaze, we are more apt to say yes to things and projects, thinking that the tasks might lead to better things, promotion, or acceptance. Sometimes they do, but what we did to get there is not enough to keep us there. Usually more is required of us. It has been my experience that out-working my white colleagues and co-workers means that I have to be the bigger person when they are promoted over me. Promotion, better things, and acceptance come from within first, and I do not have to overwork to get it. In fact, I have learned to create opportunities for leadership for myself.

Other forms of radical self-care include caring for yourself before others, setting boundaries, being authentically yourself in workplaces and elsewhere, being unapologetic about who you are, and resisting pressure to conform. As I come to practice these things, none of them cost me money, but they bring me peace and confidence, and have saved me from years of wasted time on relationships and projects that net me nothing. Reading this might make you want to call me selfish or self-centered, but I am proud that you would also have to call me well. I was unwell from all the years I had made myself a martyr for others and put their needs before my own. I now know first-hand that selflessness is not love, it is a demonstration of self-hatred.

Another way I am learning to demonstrate love for myself as I receover from assimilation is by not being so judgmental or critical of myself. Because I grew up under parental criticism, I am quick to extend grace to others when they mess up, are late or don't show up at all, say or do the wrong things, or don't uphold their word. But, when I made a mistake I would berate myself extensively to ensure that I didn't mess up again. One day I listened to my tongue lashing and realized that I was not speaking my own words but the words of my mother, and that I had picked up where she left off. After reading Dr. Thema Bryant's book *Homecoming*, I learned that I could re-parent myself. Re-parenting myself meant quite a few things, but the ones I practice now include extending grace to myself, speaking kindly to and about myself, knowing that I have a right to learn and make mistakes, showing up fully for myself, practicing discipline and diligence, and incorporating joy into as many parts of my life as I possibly can. In re-parenting myself, I realized that I didn't have to know all things at all times. I like examining situations and asking myself what I did well and what I could have done differently. It's taken a while but I am learning to see crises as opportunities for growth and promotion, and not reasons to run, hide, fall apart, or strive harder.

While re-parenting myself, it became apparent that I did not teach my three children to live and love well. When feelings of sadness and guilt arise about how I parented, I acknowledge the feelings (and try not to get wrapped up or wallow in them) as indicators that this is an area for me to continue to work on. Because I interpreted my parents' hands-off-ness as a lack of love, I chose to be a very present parent, too present. I did and fixed everything for my children, even as they became young adults. I thought I was showing love by shielding them from pain and consequences, righting their wrongs, and cleaning up (literally and figuratively) when they wouldn't. I realize now that the best parental love is a balance, not completely hands-off like my parents' but not totally hands-on like mine. I wish that early on I had the ability to discern when to do for them and when to let them do for themselves.

Another parenting blunder I made while assimilating was raising my children under the white gaze. That means I raised them to know that white people were watching them and that they needed to act accordingly. Dr. Joy DeGruy Leary discussed the phenomenon in her book, *Post Traumatic Slave Syndrome*, where ancestors taught their children to respect white people as a means of survival and this then has an impact on Black parenting today. I passed on these respectability politics to my children thinking it would help them survive and thrive in white spaces. One simple example of this is when I took my children to a store, and, like most Black parents, I reiterated the "Don't touch nothing" rule. But, I took it a step further by demanding that my children keep their hands at their sides, so that way no one could accuse them of stealing. My children spent their formative years watching white children touch everything and throw full-blown tantrums when their parents would not buy what they had in their hands. I was proud of myself and my children then, but now I realize I parented out of fear. I was too busy trying to prevent trouble when it would have been more advantageous to teach them how to manage trouble when it comes. Even now, when they are young adults, figuratively I see their hands by their sides when I wish they would put their hands on more things.

Moreover, when they were younger, my children must have felt the contradiction between hearing me tell them with my mouth that they were smart, capable, and strong, and showing them with my actions that they were fragile, incapable, and dumb. I would assign a task, verbally affirm them, and then go and complete the thing I had told them to do. Like all of us, they believed what I did and not what I said. So now, as I re-parent myself and them, I sit with the discomfort I feel when they face challenges and I reassure myself and them that they will successfully figure it out. Even when they come to dark places, and my fear for them is on 100 considering the all-time high numbers of suicide among Black young people, I have to trust them and God with the care of their lives. This is what I mean when I say love is maturity, because it takes everything I have in me to not continue to parent out of guilt and fear.

Before I knew what I now know about lovability, I believed that I was one of the most lovable people there were. I could easily be found sending greeting cards and text messages to let people know they were being thought of. When my loved ones were sick, I sent care packages which often included home-made soups, and I was the person people could count on when they fell short financially. I was forever anticipating others' needs and giving unsolicited advice about what people should do with their lives. To me, that was being a lovable person. I would have given anything to have a person like me in my life. Now that I have come to understand a bit more about lovability, I am glad to not be around the kind of person I used to be. I might have sent a card, soup, or money but when it was not acknowledged or appreciated it was the last card or gift the recipient received from me.

Practicing lovability was not intuitive and did not come easily to me. My natural inclination was to show love by what I did, and expect acts of kindness from others. But being lovable has come to mean that I need to be open. I didn't even know that I was closed, but not asking for and accepting help and trying to keep people from any inconveniences they might experience doing things for me were good examples of being closed. To become open, I practiced giving and receiving. I believed that the more open to receiving I became, the more I would attract people who would give to me. When people did things for me, I learned to sit with any discomfort I felt, reframed negative interpretations about their giving, and simply thanked them. The discomfort I felt was indicative of feelings associated with low self-worth. Moreover, where I came from if someone gave me something it usually meant they would want something from me in return. I had to trust myself to know that as an adult I could choose to be around healthier people, whereas I did not have that power in my childhood.

Another thing I learned to receive while practicing becoming lovable was badness. It was easy to associate goodness with love. Purchasing a home, getting a job with better pay and benefits, obtaining a degree, or having a child, or just waking up in the morning are good things that make me feel loved and lovable. But these things derived from the mindset I had developed wherein I believed that in order for me to be loved I had to do something. So when things went badly, I believed that I had done something wrong and it meant I was unlovable. With maturity and experience, I have come to believe that badness is just as much a part of life and love as goodness is, and that I cannot accept one without the other. As you have read thus far, I have wasted much of my life shunning and running away from pain or badness, when embracing it would have brought me to the whole and authentic life I blindly sought.

In addition to being open to receive things, I had to also practice being open to receive love. I did not know I repelled love. I began reflecting on this when I was a young divorcee, and when looking at my behaviors I recognized that unlovability showed up in my daily life. It showed up in the way I walked. I intentionally walked fast because I knew that people were less likely to stop me when I was in full stride. Plus, in my world, the sky always felt as if it was falling so my mind stayed ruminating about ways to shield myself from debris. I'm sure I walked in step with the pace of those rapid-fire thoughts. Unlovability showed up on my face. I looked unapproachable. Once when my firstborn son was a middle-schooler, I went to have lunch with him and his friends. I had a great time with them as we ate pizza and fries, and l laughed at the things they found funny. When I picked my son up from school that afternoon, I asked him what his friends thought of me. I just knew he was going to say that they found me funny and cool to be around, so I was taken aback when my son said, "They said you look angry." If a group of 12-year-old boys thought I looked angry, I can only imagine what a handful of adult men thought I looked like. Unfortunately, the few suitors who were able to get past my fast-walking and sourpuss facial expressions had another barrier to break, as my attitude was also a love repellent. Instead of seeing it as a compliment when a suitor slowed down my pace long enough to talk to me and transform my scowl into a smile, I met him with an attitude. Once while returning to work after lunch, I was in an elevator with a gentleman who watched me intently through the elevator's mirrored walls. Instead of responding to the smile on his face, I was annoyed that he stared at me without saying anything. "Do I know you?" I barked. That attitude was unwarranted and cost me an opportunity to get to know someone who could have turned out to be a great guy.

When I started working on these things, I slowed down my pace and practiced walking deliberately, assuredly, and naturally more sensually. I took time to notice my surroundings, taking in what I could see, hear, touch, smell, and taste. I smiled more and nodded at people or said hello. I gave compliments when I sincerely liked something about the person or their attire, and I slowly but painfully (due to shyness) and surely learned to make small talk by asking about the books people held in their hands or if they were having a good day. Mostly, I was met with positivity, and even when I wasn't I patted myself on the back for being and remaining open.

Personally, I did not anticipate marrying again. I had become comfortable being single and I enjoyed dating since I believed that the process would reveal evidence of my growth by the people I attracted. If I was with a person in transition, I believed it meant I too was in transition. If the person was insecure, I took it as a sign that I needed to examine myself for insecurities. Viewing dating from this perspective was less burdensome, and it was not difficult for me to let people go when their assignment had been completed. I learned some amazing things about myself from the people I dated. Had I not dated, I would have continued to believe that I had three strikes against me that prevented me from finding a mate for marriage.

I was a woman with three children, and if that wasn't

enough of a strike to run potential suitors off then my job as a mental health therapist would, and if by chance they were still interested they might change their mind when they found out I was a licensed minister of the gospel. Those were my three strikes. I wasn't looking for love though, I only wanted to repair myself. Plus, I was well aware of the so-called odds stacked against Black women who sought love. I'd heard plenty of sisters say, "Love? Good luck with that. All the fine Black men are either married, gay, in jail, or dead." So, I busied myself with juggling a career and children. I didn't go too many places, so if I couldn't find a husband at work or church, then I trusted that Jesus was the only man coming back for me.

It is interesting to note here that I have never dated a white man. As a person who had denied my Blackness and striven for white things, I am surprised at myself for never seeking to be with a white man. I do believe that racial identity development plays into partner selection and I think it would make a great study for couples who are in interracial relationships. In the Black community where colorism has long divided us, it was not uncommon for dark-skinned people to be with someone who had lighter skin for fear that their children would be too dark-skinned. The lighter-skinned person was also a symbol of status and was a power move for the partner.

Back to me, though. I had just ended a relationship I was in with an unorthodox gentleman who had untied the logic of my faulty religious and personal perspectives about sex. Although I was ready to accept that his assignment in my life had been completed, I drove to the super center to get some ice cream. I needed a tangible reward for making the hard but right decision to walk away from him. I was headed toward the Health

& Beauty aisle when I caught a glimpse of Nathan, a college classmate of mine from Appalachian State. He was reading the labels on a product he held in his hand. I scurried by before he could look up and see me. I was not in the mood for conversation. I just wanted to see if the store carried a new hair product I'd heard about and to grab some ice cream, and I was going back home to get myself together.

I was studying the shelves looking for this hair product when I saw someone out of my peripheral view walk past the aisle I was on and back up. "Well, hello there," a voice sang. I looked up to find Nathan approaching me. He was just as jovial as I remembered him being at Happy Appy, and he had aged into a distinguished-looking gentleman. In less than ten minutes we got caught up: *How are you doing? You married, got kids? What work are you doing these days? I heard you were a preacher.* There we were, both divorced, with three kids apiece—two older sons and our youngest children were girls—and both of us working to grow our businesses. "Well, it was nice catching up," I said. "I need to get back home." When I tell you that Nathan followed me around that store, I am not lying. He was right by my side telling me about his work and invited me to visit him there. He wouldn't take no for an answer, so I agreed. When I thought I finally got rid of him, he found me again in the check-out line. "You wanna go look at some houses?" he asked.

I found that to be an odd question coming from him, for so many reasons. But mostly, how would he know that driving around and looking at big houses, like I used to do with Grandma Louise in my childhood, was one of my favorite things to do? I couldn't pass it up, even though I wanted to.

Three months later we were engaged to be married. These 14 years together have been the best and hardest years of my life. With any other partner, I know I would have been a second-time divorcee. But with Nathan's nature—his goodness, kindness, patience, openness and vulnerability, idealism, tolerance and persistence—walking away would have the easiest but wrong route. Any other person would have bid me adieu as it has taken me so long to learn how to love and be lovable, and to practice openness and vulnerability. But I have to give myself credit too, because while Nathan has provided the emotional and physical safety I needed to overcome my childhood wounds, I have provided the safety and stability he needed to overcome his. I imagine that it has been just as amazing for him to watch me grow as it has been for me to watch his growth and maturity.

Today, we are an amazing family of nine—me, him, our six young adult children, and new grandson. When the kids were young we used to jokingly call ourselves *The Black Brady Bunch*, but we ditched the moniker when I stopped passing and patterning ourselves after white families. We'd learned that the proverbial white picket fence was not a means of safety and security for us but was a boundary that limited our ability to love and live freely. Life is not perfect for us, Team Summers, but we embrace and endorse the Afrocentric norms and values that kept us going early on and will keep us going until the end.

CHAPTER 10

LaTonya with a Capital T

I am happy to be Black and to be back to myself. I know the four-year-old girl in me is proud of me. I acknowledge and salute her, and I call upon her often so I remember to play and keep her childlike wonder. I refer to her as *Tannie*, a childhood name Momma Lorraine gave me. Tannie feels like home. Knowing how I feel about my names, I make a point of learning how to pronounce people's names and I call them by name when I talk to them. I often facilitate the following activity when I do diversity trainings to illustrate inclusion.

"One of the best ways you can honor a person of color is to get their name right," I said to the standing room only audience of predominantly white counselors who had registered to attend my *Impact of Power, Race, and Gender on Cross-Racial Supervisory Relationships* training at a national conference. "If you won't bother to get clients' names right, we wonder what else you might get wrong." I advanced to the next slide of my PowerPoint presentation, where *Whei* appeared on the screen. "How do you think this person's name is pronounced?" I asked, underlining it with the red beam of light coming from the

clicker in my hand. A brave soul raised their hand, "Is it pronounced *Wee*?" I shook my head and thanked the person for
their answer before I asked for another volunteer. "*Wee-eye*?"
someone offered, singing the second syllable into a question. I
thanked the person and asked for another guess. "It's *Why*, isn't
it?" I shook my head a third time, cognizant of the time and the
50 minutes I had left to teach much information. "This name
is pronounced *Way*, and it belongs to an Asian undergraduate
student who is a member of my Sister to Sister mentorship
group." I clicked my clicker and a second name appeared on
the screen, *Tabyrious*. Before I could even ask for volunteers,
someone raised their hand. "This is why I don't even try to
pronounce my clients' names," a woman in the middle of the
audience offered. "There's no way I can get that right. Instead,
I just talk to them without even trying to pronounce that. And,
to make matters worse, they want us to get their pronouns
right, too. Like she, his, theirs... I can't keep up."

I shuddered as I considered that this woman's clients wrote
out a whole check with her name on it, and she didn't even
bother to acknowledge them by name. What came out of my
mouth was much more diplomatic. "Do you mind if I ask if
you have any children?" I asked her. "Yep, two sons and they're
grown," she offered, gathering laughter from the audience.
"How long did it take you to name your firstborn?" She furrowed her brow, as if she knew where I was going. "I was going
to name him Richard, after his father. A junior, you know? And
we were all set but when he came out and I had a long look at
him, there was no way I could name him Richard. He didn't
look like a Richard. He looked like an Andrew." I thanked her

for sharing and offered that the least someone could do to honor Andrew and the story had she shared would be to acknowledge him by name. That name is legacy. I then led the group into an activity where we role-played how to ask for the pronunciation of someone's name without making it sound as if their name was a problem. "If you can pronounce pneumonia, which sounds nothing like it looks, then you can say Tah-bye-ree-uhs," I said as I red-lit the name with my clicker.

I've been called all kinds of variations of LaTonya: *Latoya, Latasha, Lat-onya*. Once a white man asked if he could call me LT. It is a display of power and privilege to nickname another person rather than try to correctly pronounce their name. Shortening and mispronouncing another's name is also evidence of an existing power differential. We can also tell where a person might be along the continuum of racial identity by their response to being misnamed. If the person doesn't offer a correction or they say, "that's fine" or "close enough," that person may be on the lower end of the continuum, as I was when I tried passing for white. A person who readily offers the correct pronunciation may be on the actualized end of the continuum. There is no reason to be offended when we are corrected; if anything, we should take offense when we are not correctable or teachable.

"I got your name from a statue in Italy," Brenda once told me, without me asking. "I thought it was the most beautiful name. Latonya Michelle. I still love it, don't you?" I spent years hoping to find that statue, and I couldn't find it anywhere online when the internet came out. I had hoped to find a magnificent white carving of a woman with a crown of flowers on her head, with maybe a cat at her feet. The closest thing I found was that Latonya is a derivative of Antonia, a common name for Roman women. So, Brenda wasn't that far off.

To me, my name had derived straight from the ghetto. Most of the Black girls I knew who were born alongside me in the 70s were given a name with a prefix of Sha-, La-, Ra-, or Ta-. The research study where people with Black-sounding names (i.e. Dwayne, Tariq, Latonya, Wei, and Roberto) received fewer call backs for job interviews they applied for than applicants with Eurocentric, white-sounding names (i.e. Hannah, Hunter, Michael, and Christopher) is well known. It is interesting to note that the study was duplicated in 2021 by researchers from the University of California, Berkeley, and the University of Chicago and the results were the same, despite Black Lives Matter and the mass hiring of chief diversity officers.

To increase their odds for upward mobility, many people of color began giving their children Eurocentric names. It is interesting to meet so many Black boys named Parker, and Black girls named Hayden. Another research study reported that while people of color with Eurocentric names were more likely to get jobs, their self-esteem and sense of self was not as high as their employed counterparts of color who had ethnic names. In other words, a Black man named Parker might get a job, but he does not have the fortitude to stay there. Dwayne, on the other hand, has the confidence in himself to endure whatever comes his way on the job.

Early in my first marriage, my then husband bought me a nameplate for the desk at my first post-graduate job. It read, *Name:* LaTonya. *Origin:* Russian-Latin. *Meaning:* Inestimable. I have loved my name ever since. Inestimable, meaning my worth cannot be estimated, or invaluable. I finally agreed with Brenda, LaTonya is a beautiful name.

I used to wonder why Grandma Louise did not change my name when she had the opportunity to do so when she adopted me. I never got the chance to ask her but later in life, I heard an adoptive parent say she kept her son's name the same because it was the biggest gift from his biological family that she could give him. I thought that was noble, and it made me appreciate my grandmother for choosing to keep my name as it was. I tucked it away as a mental note, thinking I might need it for a client or two who might consider adoption, or church members of mine if they ever sought me out for advice knowing I was adopted. I never knew the day would come when I would need what that adoptive mother gave me.

Both of my sons were in nursery school, and the firstborn was praying like crazy for a sister. I'm not talking about the now-I-lay-me-down-to-sleep prayers I was praying when I was his age. He was praying as if he knew God for himself. I would go into my prayer closet and renounce his prayers, knowing I was unmarried and celibate. I didn't want there to be any reason for him to not trust God, so I needed God to take away this desire for a sister he had.

When my firstborn was ready to enter kindergarten, I felt strongly that I should put both boys in a private, Christian school. I reasoned with myself, *You can't even pay for nursery and you want to put them in private school? This is ridiculous.* But I knew that worrying about tuition money when all I needed was an application fee, which I could afford, was pointless. I interviewed three schools, and thought it was divine intervention when I walked into Angels, the third school. I just had a good feeling about it, which I did not have at the other two. I visited the classroom where the firstborn would attend, and I noticed on the wall, among the different-colored construction paper balloons, one that read a first name I could not pronounce, but his last name was the same as my maiden name. My maiden name is less common among Black people than whites, so I knew this child was some kin to me. "Who is this kid?" I asked the teacher, pointing to the pink balloon. "That's Whanyae," she answered, with a smile. "Do you know him?" I shook my head. "No, but if he's Black, I know we're related." The teacher walked me outside where the children were playing. "He and his two brothers are in foster care, and the director of the school is taking care of them." That was confirmation. "Foster care? I know we are related." The teacher called out his name, and this dark-skinned, doe-eyed child with a wide smile ran toward us. He looked like I could have birthed him. "We are definitely related. Do you know his mother's name?" The teacher told me that she did not know, but I could talk to the director if I wanted to.

The director's office was the last stop of my tour. I was told that she would answer any questions I had about the school. I was so busy thinking about the child I saw on the playground that I'd forgotten I was there to scout the school for my own child. When the teacher and I got to the threshold of the director's door, a smiling fair-skinned woman looked up. The teacher said, "She thinks she might be related to Whanyae and his brothers. Do you know their mother's name?" The whole encounter moved in slow motion as the director spoke my first cousin's name. "That's my biological aunt's daughter. She's my first cousin." I paused, and without thinking I asked, "Will she get the boys back? If not, I want to adopt them." How I thought

I would take care of five boys, those three and my two, on my shoestring budget, was not clear. The teacher answered, "The boys are in the process of being adopted." The director added, "By a good family, too." I could have shouted with joy from the relief I felt, knowing I'd still be managing a three-person household. "Your cousin is pregnant again," the director offered. "If the baby is born under the same circumstances as the boys, the state will take that baby, too. You want to adopt it?" My first reaction was no, I'd just narrowly escaped adopting three boys. Before turning to walk away, I told the teacher and director that I'd be praying for my cousin, and I trusted that she and her new baby would be okay.

My sons loved Angels and they thrived there. One day I went to pick up the boys and the director stopped us before we could reach the door. "Your cousin had the baby," she happily announced. "Oh, that's good. How are they?" She motioned for me to walk over to her. "The state took it." My stomach dropped. "That sucks," I said. "It's a girl," the woman offered, with excitement. "I have her, you wanna see her?" That was the moment I remembered the firstborn's prayers for a sister, and my body did not know what to do in response. It did not know if it wanted to fall on my knees, break out into a praise dance, or run around the school. The moment felt so surreal, recognizing that God had answered my son's prayer. As if there was one more test this situation needed to pass, I asked what the baby's name was. If my cousin had named her firstborn Whanyae, I could not imagine what this baby had been named. "Her name is Destiny," the woman's smile broadened. Destiny means "predestined" and that's what the situation felt like, a divine and ordained one, and I did not even have to ask God what I should do. I knew I would adopt her. I did not entertain thoughts of changing her name. It was a gift for her from her mother, as she would be to me.

The adoption process took ten months. There was one glitch after the other. Destiny's father was incarcerated but he fought for his rights. We got to meet a couple of times, and I assured him that I would take care of her. After two court appointments, the judge revoked his rights since he would not be getting out of jail any time soon. Then, the social worker who was working on our case, a Black woman who was pregnant herself, died while in childbirth. Her death was soul-crushing. There I was trying to get a child I didn't carry, and she did not even get to hold her baby. I think of her often, every time I read about the disproportionate number of Black women who die from childbirthing complications. I had become so exhausted from the arduous adoption process that I didn't care how it ended, I just wanted it to be over.

Two months later, I let an older white woman social worker into my home. She had come to bring Destiny to us. "You have the same smile," she said. My smile turned downward as I studied her face, trying to remember where I knew her from. "I'm sorry, have we met before?" She laughed heartily, "Yes, we have. You were four years old when I removed you from your mother's home, and I have come to deliver your daughter. My name is Alden Davis." I may not have remembered her face, but I remembered her name, and I thanked her profusely. Unspokenly, my gratitude was for her getting me into foster care, from where I went to Grandma Louise's house, to safety. I was grateful that she was still doing her work long enough to share this moment with me. The moment was sacred. My life had come full-circle and the firstborn had got his heart's desire. That story aptly describes much of my life before I started passing, just one serendipitous moment after another. I don't know why that did not feel like enough to me.

That's the thing with racial identity development, as described by Dr. William Cross in his paper on the model of nigrescence: it is the encounters and incidents we have in life that move us along the continuum of becoming. They are not to be judged or regretted but experienced and learned from. The more mature and wiser we become from these encounters, the more anti-racist we become toward the self and others. I have become less afraid, less competitive, less judgmental, and less selfish as I have opened myself up to the full Black experience. Boldness, love, confidence, brilliance, and power—things I did not have or know I had—seem to be natural by-products of fully accepting myself.

My name is written *Latonya* Michelle on my original birth certificate. I realized that people had trouble pronouncing my first name with the lower sentence case. They approached my name as if it is one syllable. They gave up after a while, or I rescued them by pronouncing it for them. Then, because I knew a lot of white girls named Tonya, I'd say, "It's Tonya with *La* on the front." One day in my adulthood, I was writing a check to pay a bill by mail, and I drew out my signature as *LaTonya*. I *noticed* the T was capital, as it was not an intentional act. At least not that I was aware of. I liked it, the way it looked. And it solved the problem. The capitalized T seemed to readily inform people that my name was multi-syllabic. Now they easily say La-Ton-ya. I'm happy about that because I would have hated to capitalize the Y too. The thoughts folks might have about my mother, assuming she was ghetto if they saw *LaTonYa*! See how easily that white gaze comes up for me? It just goes to show that recovery from assimilation takes as much time as it took to assimilate. I passed for nearly 25 years! I cannot wait to see who I am at the end of the journey.

I may not have changed my name as Brother Ali did but I'm prepared to accept that altering my name is not that different. For me, capitalizing the T was the way I knew to take ownership of myself, my life. If the La at the beginning of my name symbolized the beginning of my life, then a capital T was symbolic of me standing up to what I'd been running from. Capitalizing the T meant accepting what my mother gave me and finding the beauty in it for myself, rather than being marred by what she did and didn't do. Moreover, the capital in the middle of my name is a huge reminder to myself to live the dash in between the dates that will be inscribed on my tombstone; to know that it doesn't matter how hard my life started out, I have the ability and power to punctuate it with as many bits and pieces of joy and love as I possibly can.

Recovering from assimilation is a daily process. Mostly for me it means that I remain conscientious about the Black gaze rather than the veil of whiteness, and focus on what it means to me knowing that Black people are not only watching me, but seeing me. It's the hope that if by any chance there are Black children or adults watching me and wanting any of the peace, confidence, resilience, or success I have gained, they see themselves in me and know that these things are there for them too. I hope that they know they are no different from me, and that they do not have to sacrifice their Blackness or themselves to obtain anything more than what they have. In fact, I hope that by seeing me they see that what they strive for or what they want is already within them. They already possess the power, courage, and wherewithal to grasp hold of what seems out of reach. If nothing else, I hope they see me and know that they too are enough, and that they are meant to be here, they belong here, and where they are is purposeful for moving them along a continuum to self-actualization, if only they will accept the encounters and learn from them.

Epilogue

Whew! You made it! You got to the end of this written journey with me. Thank you! I hope we get to meet in person so I can thank you personally. I'm a hugger (a good habit I picked up from the Black church) so prepare yourself. But, I'll be careful to ask you first as I've been trained by the counseling profession. In case we don't get to meet, I wanted to answer some questions you might have as you've read my story.

I'm blessed to still have my parents, Lorraine and Charles, with me. As they've aged they have gotten more expressive. They too have become huggers and we say "I love you" so much it seems we are making up for the times we didn't say it when I was growing up. I'm also pleased to have Brenda and Brother Ali in my life too, although sparingly and as much as my mental health permits me to engage. Of course, they too have aged and have become more sensitive. They are proud of me as their daughter. In fact, Brenda believes her "being hard" on me has led to my success. We still see the past vastly differently but

I am proud that they have forgiven themselves for our rocky past. My forgiveness process has not been linear.

Nathan and I just celebrated 12 years of marriage. The only other thing we have ever done for that length of time is parenting. We are proud of ourselves for successfully managing the storms of life, especially with my racial transformation being one of them. I came home every day with some new realization and a new fight. My emotions were all over the place, I'd be fighting mad one day, low and depressed the next, and anxious every day. His temperance and hugs sustained me. Our six young adult children are all doing well while they come to learn how to live life on life's terms. My three have had to do their own race-based healing and I am proud of their progress. Daily I ask for wisdom and courage to parent them without guilt and anxiety. That is as hard as marriage. Watching our grandchild grow is like watching the wonder of a rainbow. I feel so blessed.

My co-workers and I are doing well. The colleague whom I consider an ally and I are scheduled to run a 5k race together this weekend. It will be my first race and I appreciate her support. We continue to find things to do outside of work to improve our work relationship. Our entire department is committed to addressing race-based issues as they arise among us. We have gained enough experience to also address issues that show up among students. I love that about us and I still feel happy to be there.

I am sure you might have other questions that I did not think to answer here. I hope you will find me so I can answer you and sign your book.

Thank you again for journeying with me through this book.

I began it writing that I hoped it would be a blessing for three kinds of readers: those who have assimilated, those who want to know what life is like for those of who assimilate, and those who cannot understand why anyone would want to assimilate. I hope that each reader, even those who fall outside of my purview, has picked up something they can use to live better or help others do so. Until we meet, again, be well.

Overcoming Everyday Racism

Building Resilience and Wellbeing
in the Face of Discrimination and
Microaggressions

Susan Cousins

This enlightening and reflective guide
studies the psychological impact of racism and discrimination on BAME (Black,
Asian and Minority Ethnic) people and
offers steps to improve wellbeing. It includes definitions of race, racism and
other commonly used terms, such as
microaggressions, and evaluates the effect of definitions used to describe BAME people.

Each chapter of the book focusses on one category of wellbeing—
self-acceptance, personal growth, purpose in life, positive relations
with others, environmental mastery, autonomy—and includes case
examples, spaces for reflection and practical, creative exercises. For
use as a tool within counselling and therapeutic settings as well as
a self-help tool by individuals, each category provides a framework
for thinking about how to manage everyday racism, live with more
resilience, and thrive.

Susan Cousins is a Senior Counsellor working in Equality, Diversity
and Inclusion at Cardiff University.

£13.99 | $21.95 | PB | 224PP | ISBN 978 1 78592 850 5 | eISBN 978 1 78592 851 2

My Black Motherhood

Mental Health, Stigma, Racism and the System

Sandra Igwe

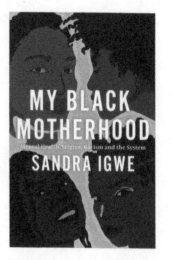

Joyful. Graceful. Blessed. Strong. Anxious. Depressed. Stigmatised. Stereotyped.

What happens when motherhood isn't what you expected—and when you reach out for support, you are met with judgment and prejudice?

Sandra Igwe shares her journey as a young Black mother, coping with sleepless nights, anxiety and loneliness after the birth of her first daughter. Burdened by cultural expectations of the "good mother" and the "strong Black woman" trope, her mental health struggles became an uphill battle.

Black women are at higher risk of developing postnatal depression but are the least likely to be identified as depressed. Sharing the voices of other mothers, Sandra examines how culture, racism, stigma and a lack of trust in services prevent women getting the help they need. Breaking open the conversation on motherhood, race, and mental health, she demands that Black women are listened to, believed, and understood.

Sandra Igwe is the Founder of The Motherhood Group, a platform and safe space to support the Black motherhood experience, through events, workshops, peer-to-peer support, collaborative projects, training, advocacy and campaigning. Sandra is co-chair of the National Inquiry into Racial Injustice in Maternity Care and a trustee of Birthrights charity.

£12.99 | $18.95 | PB | 224PP | ISBN 978 1 83997 008 5 | eISBN 978 1 83997 009 2

Black and Menopausal
Intimate Stories of Navigating
the Change
Edited by Yansie Rolston and
Yvonne Christie

"This is our voice, these are our truths, and our stories deserve to be told."

This deeply empowering and personal collection of stories brings together a wide range of Black experiences on the menopause journey. Drawing on the historical and cultural importance of storytelling traditions in African and Caribbean ancestry, this anthology breaks through a taboo topic that has too often been mired in shame and silence with courage and vulnerability.

Contributions span across various heritages, sexual orientations, ages, and gender identities, curating an intimate treasury of journeys full of honesty, pain, healing, and liberation. Topics on emotional, mental, and sexual health as well as complementary therapies are all discussed with empathy and sincerity, allowing readers to broaden their depth of understanding on the experiences of Black people impacted by the menopause.

Yansie Rolston, PhD, FRSA, is Associate Director—Health & Wellbeing at The Ubele Initiative, and Director of Efficacy EVA.

Yvonne Christie is Project Director at Efficacy EVA and Co-Founder of YouandMe Menopause. She has an MA in Applied Psychology of mental health services, a diploma in counselling and a diploma in community and youth work.

£14.99 | $22.95 | PB | 208PP | ISBN 978 1 83997 379 6 | eISBN 978 1 83997 380 2

Black, Brilliant and Dyslexic

Neurodivergent Heroes Tell their Stories

Edited by Marcia Brissett-Bailey

This is a raw, honest and enlightening collection of experiences, across the black and dyslexic community, giving an intersectional perspective on topics including the education system, the workplace, daily life and entrepreneurship. These stories highlight the challenges, progress, successes and contributions of the black and dyslexic community, helping others to find their voice, feel empowered and be proud of their differences.

It charts journeys from early childhood through to adulthood and, despite the lack of representation within the public arena, how black dyslexic people of all ages are changing the world.

Raising awareness, breaking silences and tackling the stigma around dyslexia and the difficulties stemming from a lack of support. Contributors share how they tackled their unique adversities and provide practical tips for others to live proudly at the intersection of blackness and dyslexia.

Marcia Brissett-Bailey is an inspirational speaker, co-author and passionate advocate and champion for dyslexia and neurodiversity. She was named one of the Top 50 Influential Neurodivergent Women of 2022 and was winner of the British Dyslexia Association (BDA) Adult Award 2022. Marcia was nominated for the Stereotype Buster of the Year category at the 2021 and 2022 Celebrating Neurodiversity Awards. She is a co-founder of the BDA Cultural Perspective Committee and a board member of several organisations focused on Neurodiversity.

£13.99 | $19.95 | PB | 240PP | ISBN 978 1 83997 133 4 | eISBN 978 1 83997 134 1

White Privilege Unmasked

How to Be Part of the Solution

Judy Ryde

All white people understand cultural differences from a platform of relative privilege, affecting their personal and professional interactions. How should they respond when confronted with this knowledge? This introductory book looks at the concept of whiteness, and shows how individuals can "unmask" their own whiteness and take meaningful steps to break down unconscious bias and structural racism.

Exploring how colonial history resulted in white privilege, this book examines how that privilege manifests today in a culturally diverse world, and the links between the rise in far-right politics and anti-immigration rhetoric that led to Brexit and Donald Trump's election. It looks at the pressures on privilege and white populations, with candid reflections on how even well-meaning white people may project unconscious bias in their everyday lives. There are also dedicated chapters on training to raise awareness of white privilege in professional organizations.

Judy Ryde, PhD is a freelance psychotherapist, supervisor and trainer of 25 years' experience. She provides supervision training across the helping professions within the Centre for Supervision and Team Development. Judy also supervises the BCPC Asylum Project which provides counselling and psychotherapy for asylum seekers and refugees, and was a co-founder of Psychotherapists and Counsellors for Social Responsibility.

£14.99 | $21.95 | PB | 192PP | ISBN 978 1 78450 408 8 | eISBN 978 1 78450 767 1

Jessica Kingsley
Publishers

JKP is a leading specialist global publisher at the forefront of social change. We aim to promote positive change in society and encourage social justice by making information and knowledge available in an accessible way.

Our specialist areas span autism and neurodiversity, health, social care, mental health, education, disability, gender, sexuality, and complementary health and bodywork.

We're committed to publishing books that promote diversity and inclusion, including representation of diverse race and heritage, disability, neurodiversity, gender, sexual orientation, age, socio-economic status, religion, and culture.

If you have an idea which you think would fit JKP's publishing, you can tell us about it directly by completing a proposal form at

https://us.jkp.com/pages/write-for-us